ROUTLEDGE LIBRARY EDITIONS:
EDUCATION

HAPPINESS

HAPPINESS

ROBIN BARROW

Volume 131

Routledge
Taylor & Francis Group
LONDON AND NEW YORK

First published in 1980

This edition first published in 2012
by Routledge
2 Park Square, Milton Park, Abingdon, Oxfordshire OX14 4RN

Simultaneously published in the USA and Canada
by Routledge
711 Third Avenue, New York, NY 10017

First issued in paperback 2014

Routledge is an imprint of the Taylor and Francis Group, an informa company

British Library Cataloguing in Publication Data
A catalogue record for this book is available from the British Library.

ISBN 13: 978-0-415-69581-7 (Volume 131)
ISBN 13: 978-0-415-75117-9 (pbk)

Happiness

ROBIN BARROW

Martin Robertson · Oxford

First published in 1980 by Martin Robertson & Company Ltd., 108 Cowley Road, Oxford OX4 1JF.

ISBN 0 85520 266 1 (paperback edition)
ISBN 0 85520 267 X (case edition)

Typeset by Pioneer Associates, East Sussex.
Printed and bound in Britain by Richard Clay Ltd.,
The Chaucer Press, Bungay, Suffolk.

For John Goodbody and Bruce Phillips

Now that the barbarians have got as far as Picra,
And all the new music is written in the twelve-tone scale,
And I am anyway approaching my fortieth birthday,
I will dissemble no longer.

. . .

Anyone happy in this age and place
Is daft or corrupt. Better to abdicate
From a material and spiritual terrain
Fit only for barbarians.

Roy Fuller: *Translation.*

Contents

Acknowledgement x

Introduction xi

PART I: BACKGROUND MATERIAL: EMPIRICAL, LITERARY AND PHILOSOPHICAL

1 Empirical Claims

1.1-1.3 Concerning the importance of happiness in the context of schooling 1
1.4 Views as to how to increase happiness in the context of schooling 4
1.5 A note on the problematic nature of some of the research cited 7
1.6 Psychological evidence 8
1.7 Attitudinal studies 11
1.8 Conclusion 13

2 Aristotle on Happiness

2.1-2.3 Aristotle's view of happiness in the context of his wider ethical theory 15
2.4-2.5 First problem in Aristotle's account: is happiness the sole end of human conduct? 19
2.6 Second problem: is Aristotle offering an analysis of happiness or not? 20
2.7 Third problem: does Aristotle believe that happiness is to be found only in the contemplative life? 22
2.8 Fourth problem: what is implied by the view that we should call no man happy until he is dead? 23
2.9 Conclusion 25

3 Some Literary Aphorisms

3.1-3.2 Dangers and limitations of using literary sources 27
3.3 Greek and Roman views 31
3.4-3.6 Views expressed in English literature 32
3.7-3.8 Popular non-fiction: Bertrand Russell's *The Conquest of Happiness* 36
3.9 Conclusion 39

4 The Philosophical Tradition

4.1-4.2 Epicureans and stoics to utilitarianism 40
4.3 Von Wright's *The Varieties of Goodness* 44
4.4 R. M. Hare on happiness 46
4.5 Roger Montague on happiness 47
4.6 John Wilson on happiness 48
4.7 D. A. Lloyd Thomas on happiness 49
4.8 Theodore Benditt on happiness 52
4.9 Robert Simpson and Irwin Goldstein on happiness 55

PART II: SOME POSITIVE CONCLUSIONS

5 The Concept Analysed

5.1-5.3 Different senses of the word 'happy' 61
5.4 Happiness a broad concept 64
5.5 'Happiness' a degree word 65
5.6 Happiness not to be identified with any one feeling or sensation 66
5.7 No necessary material conditions of happiness 67
5.8 No necessary personal characteristics 71
5.9 Happiness only possible for conscious beings 72
5.10 Happiness a sense of enmeshment 74
5.11 Is happiness an emotion? 75
5.12 Ascriptions of happiness are statements rather than appraisals 76
5.13 Indoctrination and happiness 78
5.14 Happiness and contentment 78
5.15 Happiness and pleasure 82
5.16 Ways in which one may be mistaken about one's happiness 83
5.17 Being and feeling happy 87
5.18 The agent the best judge of his present happiness 90
5.19 How first person expressions of doubt about happiness work 92

6 The Empirical Claims Examined

6.1-6.2 Happiness not necessarily linked to the serious and the good 94
6.3 Happiness not necessarily linked to freedom 97
6.4 Butler's 8-point plan for happiness scrutinised 98
6.5 Other proposed sources of happiness considered 100
6.6-6.7 Attitudinal research and findings reconsidered 103
6.8 Why we continue to be unhappy 107
6.9 Chemicals, drugs and neurophysical aspects of of happiness 108

7 The Value of Happiness

7.1 Happiness is an end, logically and empirically 113
7.2 Happiness the supreme end 114
7.3 The happiness of others 116
7.4 Conflicts of value 119

8 Happiness, Schooling and Education

8.1 Education not logically concerned with happiness 122
8.2 Schooling and happiness 123
8.3 Education as a source of happiness 125
8.4 Security, self-esteem and realism 125
8.5 Basic requirements 128
8.6 Dispositions conducive to happiness 130
8.7 Intellectual traits conducive to happiness 133
8.8 Ways and means: final comments 133
8.9 Conclusion 137

Notes and References 141

Select Bibliography 151

Index 157

Acknowledgement

I am indebted to the University of Western Ontario for a grant that made the writing of this book possible.

Introduction

In the first part of this book I attempt to provide a reasonably comprehensive summary of the main claims made about and on behalf of happiness, particularly in recent years. In the second part I attempt to put some shape to the material previously referred to and to draw some positive conclusions about the nature of happiness itself, some of the claims made about it and the way in which it relates to schooling and education. Although the amount of literature that I have had to examine carefully was quite considerable, I have attempted to reduce that quantity in respect of the material examined in the text, confining myself to major themes for the most part. I do not intend the book to be merely a review of the literature pertaining to happiness, but rather an examination and study of happiness and what we can confidently say about it. Naturally the material is not confined to any one discipline; indeed one of the purposes of this book (and others in this series) is to deal with issues and pursue ideas, drawing on a variety of disciplines as and when appropriate. In this case, however, the topic as a whole, including the findings and claims of various empirical disciplines, is treated philosophically in the sense that my ultimate concern and emphasis are with clarity, meaning and logic.

The first chapter introduces some of the empirical claims made about happiness, divided for convenience into claims made by educationalists, claims made by psychologists and findings reported on the strength of attitudinal studies. The object of this chapter is to be informative, and little more than an uncritical romp through the welter of suggestions made about happiness is intended. The second chapter examines Aristotle's famous contribution to the subject of happiness, while the third gathers together (without the kind of scrutiny vouchsafed to Aristotle) some of the prominent themes and views of the literary world. The fourth chapter contains a more sustained presentation of the philosophical literature on happiness, with more detailed attention being paid to the last ten years or so.

Part II begins with a positive analysis of the concept of happiness, which draws upon the material of the previous chapter. Then, now that we have a clear conception of what it is we are talking about when we use the word 'happiness', in chapter 6 the evidence and claims of chapter 1 are scrutinised and assessed. In chapter 7 the importance of happiness in general terms is established and in chapter 8 conclusions are drawn about what happiness has to do with and what it means for those concerned with the upbringing of children.

Part I is, for the most part, neutral and dispassionate in its review of the background data, while Part II seeks to argue for particular points of view. It is certainly my hope that both parts of the book will be read, but sense can be made of each part independently if need be.

PART I

Background Material: Empirical, Literary and Philosophical

CHAPTER 1

Empirical Claims

1.1 Many of the central ideas in educational theory are seen to be crucial because they are conceptually linked with education itself. For example, there is clearly some kind of logical connection between education and knowledge, and a thorough examination of the former demands close scrutiny of the latter. Other educational issues come to be regarded as crucial because they are contingently both important and problematic; moral education will serve as an example. Happiness does not obviously fit into either of these categories. It is not immediately clear that the issue of happiness, whatever the issue may be, is of pressing interest in the sphere of education in the way that moral education may be supposed to be. And it is surely certain that happiness and education are not conceptually linked. Although it might be argued that education should be pursued in some way that takes account of happiness, education does not logically imply anything about happiness and happiness does not logically imply anything about education. One can be educated and miserable, one can successfully educate someone without a thought for his happiness, one can be happy and uneducated, and so on and so forth. At any rate, if one cannot be or do any of those things, it is a contingent matter. Why, then, should the idea of happiness be of any significance to those concerned with education?

It is arguable that it should not be, but on that matter we cannot really decide until we have a clearer picture of what happiness is, what claims are made about it and what claims are made for it. What can be shown is that a great number of people, including educational theorists, philosophers, teachers, students and parents, think that in one way or another happiness is a most important consideration in the sphere of education. There is at least verbal agreement on that point, although it may well turn out that the agreement is only verbal and that different people mean different things by the word 'happiness'.

1.2 In America many educationalists refer to the clause in the Constitution that guarantees the right to the pursuit of happiness, and use that as their starting point. The Vice-President of the American Council on Education does so and argues that happiness must be pursued through the free self or as a 'function of leisure time'. 'Education's highest function', he asserts, is to enable people to 'have a creative engagement with the world of the free self', which engagement will lead to true happiness.[1] Broadus Butler, reflecting on changing ideas of happiness, suggests that America has by now substantially faced up to the challenges implicit in securing freedom, and passed on to a phase where the pursuit of happiness is of primary concern.[2] In a policy statement, the National Association for the Education of Young Children also cites the Constitution and stresses the need for schools to take great care to nurture 'life, liberty and the pursuit of happiness' since they are 'tender and vulnerable plants'. The statement adds that 'no teacher who exemplifies or risks an experience of 'death', 'constraint' and 'despair' can satisfactorily provide the necessary care'.[3] More recently, and with more swashbuckling gusto, Senator Sam Ervin has written: 'Let us take up the sword against all who imperil freedom and give them no quarter'. His thesis is that economic, personal, political, intellectual and religious freedom are essential prerequisites of the successful pursuit of happiness. Education may enhance those freedoms.[4]

In Britain the Plowden Report, though reluctant to specify its aims clearly, focusses attention on qualities such as happiness as being of signal importance in education. In the loose terminology of educational slogans the Plowden Report may be said to embody a progressive ideology, and it is perhaps not a matter of mere chance that A.S. Neill, who may also be classified as a progressive, was one of the most forthright champions of happiness as a goal. We are also beginning to amass quantified evidence relating to happiness. Ashton, for example, has shown that a large number of teachers in Britain regard it as being of prime importance as an educational goal.[5] In a review of a series of American sociological monographs,

McCord draws attention to the pervasiveness of references to happiness in educational research[6] (and the way in which its importance is taken for granted by researchers is significant), while Kramer finds that a significant number of students see personal unhappiness as their outstanding problem.[7] Certain philosophers too have argued that happiness and education are closely linked. Jeremy Bentham stated that 'the common end of every person's education is Happiness'.[8] James Mill claimed that 'the end of Education is to render the individual as much as possible an instrument of happiness, first to himself and next to other beings'.[9] In a recent paper Lewis Rutherford echoes that thought, while suggesting that for Aristotle and Dewey, too, happiness had seemed a crucial concern of education.[10]

1.3 Happiness then is widely taken to be a matter of considerable educational importance. That gives rise to the question of the presumed nature of the relationship between happiness and education, which might take many forms. It might be argued that the main thing is that children should be happy at school, perhaps on the grounds that that is in itself good, perhaps on the grounds that a happy environment is more productive in terms of various other educational objectives. Some such view seems to be implicit in much progressive literature. Or it might be argued that education should consist in whatever is most likely to enhance the long-term future happiness of the individual. It might be claimed that true education will automatically enhance the individual's happiness. Thus Plato clearly expected the fully educated philosopher-kings in his ideal state to be the happier for their education, just as Rousseau expected the very different type of education he proposed for Emile to make him happy.[11] Others apparently see education as at least necessary to complete happiness: Bailey claims that 'we know that lasting inner satisfactions come from four sources: creating and appreciating beauty, enhancing physical satisfactions, performing obligations of service, and intensifying intellectual and emotional discovery'.[12] He concludes that education, understood as the attempt to open up those sources to the individual, is indispensable as a means to happiness. Yet again, some might see Neill's claim that happiness is the aim of life[13] (i.e. some ultimate moral and social value rather than merely an educational objective) as leading to the conclusion that schools should take whatever steps are likely to maximise the general happiness of society as a whole.

On the other hand there are those who would argue that happiness cannot properly speaking be an aim of education at all. That view might be held essentially because of the practical consideration that such an aim is too abstract and remote from the daily task of teaching to make it meaningful to adopt it as an aim. Alternatively it might be held on the grounds that happiness is not something that you can educate for: happiness, it might be said, is a matter of temperament or disposition, and it is not the kind of thing that education can touch. However that may be, it is worth pointing out here that, even if it is true that education as such cannot do much for happiness, it is still possible that schooling may have an important part to play in respect of happiness. I take schooling to be a much broader notion than education, such that education certainly is, and perhaps rightly is, only a part of schooling.

1.4 The question of the relationship between happiness, education and schooling is not the only one that needs exploring. We also need to try and sort out such problems as whether happiness *does* matter as much as is being claimed, why we fail, in so far as we do, to promote it, and what kind of solutions would be appropriate to increasing happiness in whatever ways are thought desirable. Most of these are ultimately empirical questions and there has not been a great deal of satisfactory research in this area.

The educational literature relating to happiness is distressingly prone to making claims without any backing. For example, Papadatos asserts that most schools have the wrong colour schemes. He advocates bright coordinated colour schemes as being most productive of happiness. But the evidence for this, at least as presented, is practically non-existent. He writes that 'colors have profound psychological effects upon employees in industry' as 'studies have shown'; but he does not cite any such studies. The only evidence Papadatos does cite are unattributed comments from various school superintendents in New York and Connecticut, such as this one: 'It is my belief that those who utilise these kinds of colorful facilities can be more creative, more productive and happier'.[14] Perhaps the superintendent in question assumes that, provided the colours promote creativity, they are bound to promote happiness, on the grounds that increased creativity leads to greater happiness. That is the view of Gordon MacLeod.[15] Other suggestions to be found in the educational literature include: that we deny ourselves happiness because we have trivialised our society; that we confuse the egocentric pursuit of pleasure with the pursuit of happiness, which is something quite different; and, as I have already noted, that we need happy teachers, if we are to bring up a happy generation of children.

Slightly more organised research suggests that the strain imposed by academic fears may be a major factor in diminishing immediate student happiness.[16] Further problem areas for most people seem to be financial affairs, sex, love and relationships with parents. There is some evidence about religion that suggests a significant relationship between religious ritual (rather than faith) and happiness.[17] There is also increasing evidence and speculation in the physiological domain, typical of which is Evans' reminder that we are now faced with the possibility of mind-altering drugs that can induce happiness.[18] Research such as this raises a host of interesting questions, conceptual, ethical and educational: would drug-induced feelings really be happiness? ought we to induce happiness by such means? would the inducing of happiness in this way have anything to do with education?

There is a strong temptation amongst educationalists to identify an increase in happiness with breaking away from traditional academic schooling. The view that increased emphasis on creative activity would increase happiness has already been referred to. What I have loosely characterised as progressive ideology sees important links between happiness and such things as freedom, self-direction and discovery. There is, besides, the plausible claim that happiness and self-esteem are closely connected, and the consequent assumption that the child's self-esteem is more important than his success on some predetermined scale — the view, in fact, that it is more important that the child should *feel* he is doing well by his own criteria than that he should *be* doing well by different criteria imposed by the teacher.

But a number of Americans, while characteristically retaining an emphasis on freedom, do not feel drawn to advocate much increased freedom in the classroom. 'Few human experiences', according to Bailey, 'can match in sheer exhilaration the rewards of the cultivated human mind at play and at work along the frontiers of its capacity',[19] and he goes on to suggest, though not perhaps too clearly, that it is in the study of literature that our greatest hope for happiness may lie. Nor is he alone in his conviction that human happiness is intimately connected with the business of making and remaking choices and commitments. Broadus Butler holds a similar view, and he also strikes a familiar note with his cry that happiness is disappearing owing to the general breakdown of society. 'We must return through history to the words of William Ellery Channing who understood the pursuit of happiness to be the search for perfection of human nature in order to realise what are its highest possibilities.' In Butler's view the restoration of a sense of belonging (to family, peer group, community and country) is essential to happiness.[20]

Further ideas worth drawing attention to without critical comment at this point are: that we need to reawaken a sense of responsibility in people to increase their happiness;[21] that children need to learn discipline, control and the 'ability to find satisfaction through [their] understanding';[22] that there is evidence that human irrationality, in the sense of the tendency to indulge in behaviour that leads to significant interference v ith happiness, may be biologically based and as such ineducable;[23] that only by offsetting the collectivist totalitarian tendency of education can we achieve the true goal of education, which must 'not be to alienate man from his existential roots but to make him able to pursue happiness through desocialising and desociologising our schools';[24] that comparative study of a sample of Chinese and a sample of Americans indicates that the latter experience greater intensity of misery and joy, while the former experience a more constant mild equilibrium - a difference that may be attributed, the researcher hypothesises, to the difference between the individual-centred upbringing of the Americans and the social-centred upbringing of the Chinese;[25] that children might be encouraged to engage in a simulation game focussing on the theme of happiness.[26]

Perhaps the most interesting specific pedagogic idea for happiness is the Unself programme advocated by William Strong. The term 'unself' is coined to stress the non-otherness of society, the idea being to destroy the allegedly dangerous myth of the isolated self, so much beloved of literature. Basically 'unself' implies commitment, which is to be distinguished from fanaticism. But in its full flowering it involves 'sharing through patterned action' (which is somewhat obscure) and is 'closely linked with the notion of unselfishness'. As I understand the concept, it has close ties with empathy. Strong's most interesting contribution, however, is to be found in his tips for developing unself. He sees role-playing exercises as important and also suggests that raising questions about people's values and the exploration of the significance of rituals and events might prove useful. 'The focus of unself study at all times is . . . overcoming separateness through various kinds of outward turning.' Through such study, it is claimed, happiness may be increased.[27]

1.5 Most of the material to which I have so far referred is of North American origin, and that is a true reflection of the North American dominance of the literature generally. Reasons might be hazarded as to why North Americans should, overtly at least, be so much more concerned about happiness than British or European educationalists: is it perhaps a consequence of the ever-present reminder in the Constitution? is it that they are more democratic in spirit and less preoccupied with certain traditional academic aspects of education that may seem tinged with élitism? or might it be that they have a more vivid sense of losing control of society and of alienation, and consequently are more agitated about happiness themselves? (Research indicates that levels of reported unhappiness in the United States are comparatively high.[28]) Whatever the reason, we are obliged to concentrate largely on North American research.

I shall be looking more closely and critically at some of the points raised in the previous sections in chapter 6. For the moment the thing to note is the problematic nature of much of the research cited. In the first place, by and large, it is reflective and speculative, rather than systematically and scientifically researched. An extreme example is afforded by a series of short articles published in the *Humanist* in which various individuals write about how they found happiness. An instance is Craig Mosher's 'Woodworker', which might be described as a brief essay on the theme 'How I left the rat race and found happiness as an independent craftsman'. Mosher is perfectly sensible, and he offers some quite plausible suggestions as to why he is happier now than previously (e.g. he is his own boss, he can take pride in his work, he can vary what he does); but the net result does not amount to much more than the familiar saws of folk-wisdom.[29] There is nothing wrong with folk-wisdom in itself, but it cannot satisfy the yearning for hard evidence and well-attested laws. To a lesser degree, most of the research cited fails to satisfy that yearning. A second, more particular problem is to be found in the lack of agreement and lack of clarity about what happiness is. Although everybody purports to be talking about the same thing (viz: happiness), it is highly unlikely that they actually are. Bailey, at one extreme, indicates that he has an Aristotelian conception that makes happiness 'a felicitous inner condition achieved by purposive activity'.[30] At the other extreme Kramer identifies it with people feeling alright.[31] What, say, Papadatos (the colour enthusiast) means by it is nowhere revealed. Not only do we need to know what a given individual says he means by happiness, and to recognise that different people may mean different things, we also, very often, need to explore the concept further to ensure that we really understand what is said. When all is said and done, what *is* 'a felicitous inner condition achieved by purposive activity' and how does it differ from 'feeling alright'? Thirdly, once we have a grasp of the individual's conception, there is the question of how that conception affects that individual's argument or research. Quite often it seems to transpire that the claim being made is trivially true, because it has been made true by definition (this, I shall suggest below - 6.5, is the case with MacLeod's thesis that creativity is necessary to happiness); sometimes it seems that the claim made, though possibly true, just isn't about happiness as most of us understand that term: this may be the case with the claim that happiness can be induced by drugs; and some conceptions of happiness would seem to rule out in advance the possibility that one could be happy watching television or gazing at a beautiful landscape. We have to ask whether that is acceptable to our commonsense. Finally, once the conceptual problems are sorted out, there remain the classic problems of whether the evidence is adequate, the research reliable and the argument strong and acceptable in each case.

1.6 For convenience I have drawn a distinction between the educational research and the psychological research on happiness (which will be the subject of this section), although the two constantly interweave in practice. The psychological research is, generally speaking, more systematic, if no less vulnerable to searching criticism.

Balinsky and Finkelman[32] draw a distinction between (1)

happiness considered as a temperament or disposition, picked out by the description of a person as cheerful, sanguine, depressed, etc., (2) happiness considered as a mood, picked out by the attribution of cheerfulness, depression, etc. to an individual, and (3) happiness considered as an emotion, picked out by reference to the phenomenon of laughing, feeling angry, etc. (i.e. We may describe an individual as a happy sort of person referring to his disposition; we may refer to the mood of happiness that currently engulfs him; or we may pinpoint the emotion that, in his happy state, he feels.) The terminology is, to say the least, debateable, and we shall need to consider the question of what an emotion is below (5.11). But for our immediate purposes the distinction is useful and enables us to point out that most of the research is concerned with happiness considered as a temperament in their sense.

Landry finds that for children given a 'self-concept enhancement programme' there are 'very significant increases on the factor scales of happiness, sociability [and] sharing'.[33] In other words, and there is further research to support this, self-esteem and happiness are importantly related: one way of increasing happiness is to increase self-esteem. Jokiel claims there is evidence for a rather more prosaic link between pleasant school surroundings and situations and happiness, (not, however, between success and happiness.)[34] But most of the limited evidence we have about causes of happiness comes from research into job satisfaction. And, despite certain obvious problems in such research, such as that the job satisfaction of an individual may relate as much to the importance the job has for him as to any variables within the job, some interesting suggestions do emerge.

Of variables within the job themselves there is evidence that some affect the agent's satisfaction more than his dissatisfaction, and that others affect dissatisfaction more than satisfaction. For example, it is argued, according to the two-factor theory of Herzberg, that certain kinds of variable such as holiday arrangements may cause dissatisfaction if they are unsuitable or inadequate, but not materially increase satisfaction if they are suitable and adequate. The division is between *motivators,* which are intrinsic to the job and provide satisfaction (e.g. recognition, responsibility, advancement), and *hygeines* which are extrinsic and can cause dissatisfaction (e.g. hours of work, supervision, holiday arrangements). These findings, in so far as they are well-founded, could have interesting repercussions for attempts to increase children's satisfaction in school. (There is also evidence to support the view that positive reinforcement, e.g. rewards, praise, is more efficacious than negative reinforcement, e.g. punishment.) Assuming that the distinction between *motivators* and *hygeines* is legitimate, it follows that motivators have to be in order or satisfactory for there to be any chance of job satisfaction: the scope for recognition, responsibility and advancement must be judged to be adequate by the employees.[35]

There is, in addition, research that claims that it is important for job satisfaction that the individual's intelligence should be neither too great nor too small for the work in question. But an interesting question then arises: are people satisfied because they are good at their jobs, or, rather, good at their jobs because they are satisfied? Katzell claims that the quality or calibre of work has nothing to do with satisfaction, but that the quantity of work (i.e. busyness, output) does. Vroom, however, thinks the evidence suggests that good performance (which might be judged quantitatively, but equally well might not) leads to satisfaction.[36] If opinion seems divided on that matter, there is at least general agreement amongst psychologists that authoritarianism is inimicable to happiness. In sum it seems that 'job satisfaction is probably the result of interactive influence of personality and environment factors'[37] and that people are happy at work if matters intrinsic to the job are satisfactory, if they do the job well, if their self-esteem is high and if they are not subject to authoritarianism.

A natural everyday assumption might well be that if you are tired, hurt or sick, you will be the unhappier for it, whereas the climate and physical surroundings cannot really make you more or less happy. Young, however, argues that the environment is a more important consideration in affecting mood than bodily state.[38] More generally, W. Wilson studied the available psychological literature and came to the conclusion: 'The happy person emerges as a young, healthy, well-educated, well-paid, extroverted, optimistic, worry-free, religious, married person with high self-esteem, high job morale, modest aspiration, of either sex and a wide range of intelligence.'[39] To that interesting summary we shall return (6.7), as we shall to Scott's view on certain active steps we could take to make people happy (8.9). He claims that 'an individual forms habits of not fighting simply by not fighting in particular situations' and similarly with other agonistic behaviour.[40] Therefore, in so far as fighting or any other such behaviour is inimical to happiness, we have merely to train it out. There is evidence that early conditioning may lead to the easy acceptance of domination, and for the value of games in channelling aggression out; also that physical restraint is more effective as a long-term deterrent than punishment. But the most important claim here is that internal reaction can and should be conditioned in harmony with external reactions: that the tendency to strike back can be controlled as well as the action.

1.7 A great deal of the psychological literature relating to happiness takes the form of attitudinal studies. This research deserves to be categorised separately since it has its own problems and limitations. The fact that so much of the research into happiness does take the form of surveying and inquiring into people's attitudes, as perceived by themselves, should surprise no one. That kind of research can at least be done, whereas attempts to measure happiness itself or locate happiness feelings would seem a somewhat daunting task. But that does not mean that attitudinal studies are straightforward. On the contrary, they are fraught with difficulties: are the researchers clear about what they are asking about? can they guard against tautology in their questions? are the subjects clear in their own minds and are they talking about the same thing as the researchers? The trouble is that the more sophisticated the instrument, the more subtle the concepts and questions involved, the greater the danger of clumsy responses, distortion and confusion. The brute fact is that questions of the type 'In general how satisfying do you find the way you're spending your life these days' are not simple and straightforward to answer, and will be interpreted in different ways by different people. Furthermore there is a list of further difficulties inherent in any questionnaire-based inquiry, and particularly in those that ask people to make judgements about themselves. Are people honest? do people deceive themselves? do they understand the question as it was intended they should? are the questions adequate to the task in hand? is the sample representative? Take, for example, these items where the subject is asked to express his agreement or disagreement: 'I don't seem to have very much respect for myself'; 'I feel sour and pessimistic about life in general'; 'in almost every respect, I'm very glad to be the person I am'. Is it easy to rate one's degree of agreement or disagreement with those propositions? Are we confident that our response operates in the same way and on the same scale as that of other people? Are you a person who never/seldom/sometimes/often or very often 'feels he must win an argument'? Perhaps you don't really know, because perhaps you don't realise that it is a desire to win the argument that often motivates you. Perhaps you and I would assess our fear of 'trying something new' differently, simply because we interpret 'fear' and 'trying something new' in different ways. One actual example will suffice to make the point. Lenski and Leggett found that more than two-thirds of their respondents who agreed with the statement 'It's hardly fair to bring children into the world, the way things look for the future', also agreed that 'Children born today have a wonderful future to look forward to'.[41]

Caution is obviously needed. But assuming we exercise caution in accepting the findings, we may say that the main thrust of the research is as follows:

According to Wessman's 1956 research, levels of reported unhappiness are highest in France, followed by Canada, the United States, England and Holland, in that order.[42] In percentage terms, according to a 1951 survey, about 9 per cent of Americans, 6 per cent of British and 13 per cent of Canadians regarded themselves as not happy.[43] Rescher, studying the data concerning Americans between 1946 and 1965, argues convincingly that during that period there was a small but perceptible increase in unhappiness. He points out that not only do attitudinal reports show that by 1965 17 per cent of the sample reported themselves as not happy, but also suicide figures remained more or less constant and admissions to mental hospitals had increased.[44]

Certain correlations seem reasonably well established: unhappiness repeatedly shows a significant correlation with alienation, depression, anxiety and anomie. Happiness shows a significant correlation with self-esteem, successful involvement with other people and social adjustment. (It is also worth noting that anomie is to be found to a great degree in low-cognitive, inflexible and extremist individuals, while sense of self-worth and trust of others appear to go hand in hand.) Such correlations may prove useful in helping us to assess ways in which to preserve and increase people's happiness. No less useful will be other research relating to causes or sources of happiness and unhappiness. According to Cantril, two-thirds of us see economic factors as crucial in a good and satisfactory life; half regard health and family contentment as important. Work and the international political situation, on the other hand, rank low amongst our concerns, while social values and domestic politics rank lower still. However, poor health is generally considered the most damaging feature of life, which suggests that, since only a quarter of the sample noted family concerns in connection with the worst possible life, 'one's family is far more likely to be thought of as a source of hopes rather than fears, the international situation having the opposite function'. Over 40 per cent of the sample maintained that 'lack of training and education' kept them from having a more satisfactory life. There does not appear to be a significant correlation between any particular activities and happiness, but there is evidence that people who spend more time in leisure activities of some sort are happier. More generally it seems that status may affect one's happiness to a significant degree.

When it comes to the question of what kind of people find happiness the evidence is similarly suggestive but inconclusive. There appears to be no crucial difference between the sexes, although single men tend to be more unhappy than single women and 'all studies indicate married people to be significantly happier than unmarried people'. Students appear to be a particularly dissatisfied group, while high achievers (i.e. those whose income outstrips their qualifications) and 'persons of higher social status' invariably report higher levels of satisfaction. Low achievers, people of low capability and divergent people report low levels of satisfaction. There are particular problems in assessing relative happiness levels between negroes and whites, but all American studies except two suggest that 'roughly twice as high a proportion of Negroes as Whites report themselves as not too happy or not very satisfied'.[45]

1.8 So much for the empirical literature. Even if we put aside queries about the reliability of the research and the value of its findings, a number of important questions remain: what is the explanation of these various facts? could they be altered if we wanted them to be? if so, in what way? with a matter like happiness are people's attitudes as important as the objective facts of the case? can such a distinction be drawn? But behind all such questions there lies another: what is happiness? Until we have some clear answer to that we are in no position to answer the other questions or to assess the significance of the empirical research.

CHAPTER 2

Aristotle on Happiness

2.1 It is difficult to avoid mention of Aristotle when discussing happiness, particularly when considering the question of what it is or what it consists in. He was not the first person to take happiness seriously; as he himself points out, in his own society it was a commonplace that happiness was a good. But he was the first to attempt a systematic examination of the notion of happiness and to raise such questions as what is necessary to it, how may we best achieve it and whether we should pursue it and it alone. The influence of his account, to be found for the most part in the first and last books of his *Nichomachean Ethics,* has been enormous.[1] In the philosophical literature his influence has been explicitly recognised. But in less specialist circles too he leaves his mark: Stephen Bailey's definition of happiness as 'a felicitous inner condition achieved by purposive activity', noted in the previous chapter, is more or less identical with Aristotle's claim that happiness is 'an activity of the soul in accordance with virtue'; the view that happiness lies in a life of moderation, the view that friendship is crucial to happiness, the view that ideally man's happiness should be achieved through intellectual pursuits, and the observation that 'one swallow doesn't make a summer' - all are expounded and explored in Aristotle.

2.2 Aristotle's account of happiness is interwoven with his wider ethical theory and view on the nature of man. He argues that human beings are essentially purposive creatures who act with an end in view; furthermore whatever end we adopt at any given time will be something that seems to us to be desirable or good, although the means that we then adopt are not necessarily regarded by us as desirable in themselves; they need only be seen as good for the purpose of achieving the end. Now of course what serves as a means to some end on one occasion might itself be treated as an end on another. (Today I am reading in order to find something out; tomorrow I may read for its own sake.) Conversely, the end of my present action might subsequently serve as a means to another end. But Aristotle thinks that, though for the most part we adopt and discard immediate ends at will, there must logically be some one final end, not in the sense of an end that is as a matter of fact always at the end of a given chain of reasoning, but in the sense of an end that is always and only chosen as an end, never as a means. It is possible for human beings to go through life more or less aimlessly, but Aristotle urges that they should take positive steps to live well; that they should have a plan of life. Given the assumption of a final end, this means that ideally they should adopt the *plan* of life that involves reference to *the* final end. What that end is can easily be stated, in words at least. It is *eudaimonia,* conventionally translated happiness. Man should seek to *eu prattein,* live or fare well, and thus experience *eudaimonia.*

But the question now arises as to whether it is appropriate to regard this plan of life as *the* one plan aiming at *the* one end. Surely, it may be thought, different people may acquire their happiness in different ways, they may have different ideas of what is involved in living well. Isn't happiness just a matter of getting what you want? And doesn't that put an end to Aristotle's idea of there being one and only one way to live?

Aristotle himself, while being well aware of the undeniable fact that different people seek happiness in different ways, thinks not. He points out that there is a distinction to be drawn between natural and acquired desires or needs and wants. Natural desires are desires for things that men need in virtue of being what they are. For example, men need or have a natural desire for food, shelter, air and reasoning. Our existence is dependent on the fulfilment of such desires. But there are other things that we desire because of the kind of life we want to lead or are used to. We need food of some sort to survive, but we may want cooked food as opposed to raw food because we are used to it or conditioned to it. It is an acquired desire. The distinction between natural and acquired desires does not depend upon such factors as the intensity of our longing for something or our awareness of its absence. A baby needs food, even though he is not aware of that need; in Aristotle's terminology he has a natural desire. Conversely, the drug addict, though he craves for his drugs, does not need them; he has an acquired desire for them. On this account needs are by definition always good, and Aristotle makes the further distinction between real goods for man – which are those things we need and for which we have a natural desire (food, drink and, in Aristotle's view, knowledge) – and apparent goods – those things we may want or for which we may have acquired desires, but which are not necessarily good for us.

Aristotle's argument is that happiness is dependent on seeking and acquiring real goods (although he allows in addition that we may require our various wants satisfied too, provided that satisfying them does not prove injurious to ourselves or others), and consequently, since these real goods are linked to needs that stem from human nature and are the same for all, it transpires that the path to happiness is essentially the same for each person. More substantive detail is provided when Aristotle proceeds to indicate what these real goods are, under various headings. First, there are certain biological goods that are necessary for living and hence for living well: food, drink, clothing and shelter. Second, we require the bodily goods of health and the satisfaction of some bodily pleasures. Third, the external good of wealth is necessary at least up to a point, as a means to ensure some of the other goods. Finally, since man is by nature a questioning, thinking, knowing animal, his happiness is also linked to certain goods of the soul such as knowledge, friendship and self-respect.

One thing more, one rather surprising thing perhaps, is needed to ensure happiness in Aristotle's view, and that is the development of a good moral character so that the individual can be relied upon to behave habitually in a moral fashion. Aristotle's reasoning here appears to be that in practice the above goods will not be attainable except through the habitual exercise of virtue. This becomes clearer when one appreciates that by virtuous behaviour Aristotle means behaviour that consists in making the correct choice between real and apparent goods, or in pursuing the mean between extremes that are equally detrimental to man's real interest. (Thus, temperance consists in displaying the amount of restraint that man needs to display; courage is to be identified not with blind foolhardiness but with a proper degree of resolution; justice involves steering expeditiously between the extremes of selfishness and altruism.)

Virtuous behaviour, in this sense, will not guarantee happiness, since there is still an element of luck or fortune at play, as Aristotle admits. But he thinks it a necessary condition of living the kind of practical life that will ensure the real goods that are necessary for happiness. Finally, he claims that the surest path to happiness lies in going beyond the life of practical virtue to the contemplative life or the life of *theoria*.

Aristotle's basic claims, then, would appear to be as follows:[2] Happiness is the highest of all goods attainable by effort (1095 a 14); it is an end that is unique in that of all the ends that man may adopt this alone is always chosen for its own sake and never as a means to some other end (1097 b). Happiness arises out of (or consists in) the active pursuit of virtue over a complete lifetime (1097 b 22). It is not to be found in idle amusement or in the pursuit of isolated pleasures (the libidinous life), or in the pursuit of honour, even if successful (the political life). In fact, man being a rational, theoretical or contemplative creature, true human happiness lies in the contemplative life (which should be understood to subsume the satisfaction of more worldly desires and the successful practical life). Most men, however, being incapable of attaining the contemplative life, will have to be content with the secondary degree of happiness that accompanies the successful life on the practical level (1178 a 8).

In addition Aristotle makes the following points: He clearly acknowledges that wealth, honour and the satisfaction of acquired desires may contribute to happiness (1095). He sees a need for basic security provided by external goods and remarks that 'those who say that the victim on the rack or the man who falls into great misfortune is happy if he is good, are talking nonsense' (1153 a). He argues that friendship is necessary to happiness on the grounds that 'man is a political creature and one whose nature it is to live with others' (1169 b). He claims that animals and children cannot strictly speaking be called happy, on the grounds that they are not capable of performing good and noble acts or of engaging in the contemplative life (1100 a). And he believes that 'no supremely happy man can ever become miserable . . . [for being] truly good and wise he will bear all kinds of fortune in a seemly way'. Misfortune may prevent him being accounted truly blessed, but by making the best of his circumstances, 'even as a good general makes the most effective use of the forces at his disposal', he will retain his happiness (1101 a).

2.4 It is now necessary to raise four important questions about the interpretation of Aristotle's view. The first is the question of whether he does or does not believe that happiness is the sole end of human conduct. The second concerns the nature of what he says about happiness: should we construe it as an analysis of what happiness is, or as a statement of the causes and/or sources of happiness? The third is whether he does or does not think that the happiness to be found in the contemplative life is the only true happiness. Finally there is the question of precisely what significance we should attach to Aristotle's stress on the qualification 'in a complete life' and his assertion that we should call no man happy until he is dead.

2.5 Does Aristotle consider happiness to be the single supreme end of action in the sense of being the thing for the sake of which ultimately we do everything? The passage that particularly gives rise to the view that he does is this:

> If, then, there is some end of the things we do, which we desire for its own sake (everything else being desired for the sake of this), and if we do not choose everything for the sake of something else (for at that rate the process would go on to infinity, so that our desire would be empty and vain), clearly this must be the good and the chief good.[3]

Both Anscombe and Geach argue that Aristotle here seeks to prove that there is only one end, and that he fails, since the argument contains 'an illicit transition' from 'all chains must stop somewhere' to 'there is somewhere where all chains must stop'.[4] Most commentators on the other hand assume that Aristotle only wants to assert that man must have some ends, and that happiness is one such end.

It is certainly true that Aristotle recognises that man may adopt other ends besides happiness; for example, pleasure and honour (1097 b). But it is surely also clear from the passage cited that he contemplates the possibility of a supreme end (supreme but not sole). Furthermore that suggestion is confirmed by the previous observation that 'if there is only one final end, this will be what we are seeking . . . the practical good or goods, if there are more than one'. He immediately goes on to draw a distinction between things that may be chosen as means, although they can be ends, and something final: 'So if there is only one final end, this will be the good for which we are searching; if there are more than one, it will be the most final of these.' That last curious phrase strongly implies that Aristotle is determined, one way or another, to isolate one ultimate or supreme end. He proceeds by explaining that that which is always chosen as an end is 'more final' than that which is also sometimes chosen as a means. Presumably it is conceivable that there might be more than one 'more final' end in this sense, but Aristotle appears to think that, whether there might be or not, there are in fact not.

In my view, then, Aristotle thinks that happiness is unique in being an end always chosen only for its own sake, never as a means to something else, and that it is therefore supreme among other ends that may on occasion be adopted. He remarks that

> happiness more than anything else is thought to be just such an end [more final], because we always choose it for itself and never for any other reason. It is different with honour, intelligence and good qualities generally. We choose them [sometimes] for themselves, but also sometimes for the sake of happiness. [1097 b]

The strong implication is that this is true of everything except happiness. The conclusion that 'happiness is found to be something perfect and self-sufficient, being the end to which our actions are directed' I take to mean that, of the various ends we may choose to adopt, only happiness is always chosen for its own sake, only happiness is enough in itself to constitute a completely satisfactory end, and happiness is really what we are always ultimately aiming at, even though at a given time our conscious self may concentrate on some less final end.

2.6 The second problem in interpreting Aristotle is more far-reaching. It is the question of whether we should take him to be offering an analysis of happiness (indicating the various conditions that make happiness happiness) or making comments about sources and causes of happiness (indicating what as a matter of fact makes men happy). The weight of contemporary opinion favours the former view, but there have been some powerful voices, such as that of

Prichard, raised on the other side.

At the beginning of the *Nichomachean Ethics* Aristotle remarks that 'so far as the name goes there is pretty general agreement [as to what is the highest good]: it is *eudaimonia*', according to both ordinary people and educated people. And they likewise agree in identifying *eudaimonia* with living and doing well. 'But when it comes to saying what *eudaimonia* is, opinions differ.' Some people, he goes on to point out, identify it with pleasure, some with wealth, some with honour and others with health. In contradistinction to such views Aristotle then offers his own, at this stage tentative, view that happiness is 'an activity of the soul in accordance with virtue . . . in a complete lifetime'.

It is in reference to the above line of argument that Prichard makes the following comment:

> He [Aristotle] certainly did not think that anyone ever meant by *eudaimonia* either honour or wealth; and he certainly did not himself mean by it activity of the soul in accordance with complete virtue. What he undoubtedly meant and thought others meant by the word *eudaimonia* is happiness. Plainly too what he thought man differed about was not the nature of happiness but the conditions of its realisation and when he says that *eudaimonia is* activity of the soul in accordance with complete virtue, what he really means is that the latter is what is required for the realisation of happiness.[5]

To that crisp statement Hardie rejoins that

> if we say that a philosopher 'really means' something which he has not said we imply that what he has said is, as it stands, so absurd or so obviously false that, when this is pointed out, the need for a revised statement will be admitted. I can see no such absurdity in what Aristotle says here.[6]

He also argues that Prichard has misunderstood Aristotle's account of the nature of 'what is' questions, as given in the *Posterior Analytics*.[7] According to Prichard, Aristotle sees a scientific definition of *X* as stating only the condition(s) necessary for its realisation. Thus 'quenching of fire in clouds' serves as a definition of thunder. Hardie correctly points out that Aristotle actually expects a definition to state the genus as well as the differentia. That is to say, the full definition of thunder should be '*noise* produced by quenching of fire in clouds'. If that is so, Prichard's claim that the question 'what is *eudaimonia*?' is to be interpreted as meaning 'what are the conditions necessary for its realisation?' is to be rejected.

However one might reasonably suggest that Aristotle regards *eu prattein* ('faring well') as constituting the genus in question. Thus in full his question 'what is *eudaimonia*?' means 'what are the conditions necessary for the realisation of *eu prattein* which provides happiness?', just as 'what is thunder?' means 'what are the conditions necessary for a particular kind of noise?' Aristotle might well be saying that all mankind agree that the supreme good is *eudaimonia,* which is a species of well-being; the question about which there is disagreement is what leads to *eudaimonia.* That interpretation is certainly supported by the fact that some at least of what Aristotle goes on to say can only reasonably be construed as comment about happiness and how to acquire it. (For example, he remarks that some people identify happiness with good fortune (1099 b 7). But strictly speaking nobody would *identify* happiness with good fortune; nobody would say one means the other or even logically entails the other. What many people might do is regard the attainment of happiness as a matter of good fortune.)

If there is any truth in Prichard's view, it is ironic that Aristotle should be so consistently referred to in the philosophical literature on happiness, since that view involves the claim that the one thing he failed to do was analyse the concept. For our immediate purposes the important thing is to recognise that at best Aristotle does not seem to be clear about the distinction between the question of what happiness is and the question of what conditions are necessary for its realisation. That distinction must be clearly made in our own case.

2.7 The third problem lies in the fact that he appears to some commentators to contradict himself between books 1 and 10 of the *Nichomachean Ethics.* In Book 1 he seems to say that happiness for man lies in the practical life; to be specific, it is the outcome of activity in accordance with virtue. In Book 10 he says, unambiguously, that true happiness is to be found in the contemplative life.

Despite the fact that many find this an awkward disjunction, I am inclined to follow Broyer in thinking the disharmony more apparent than real.[8] Aristotle's view is that, given that man is part instinctive, part practical and part contemplative, complete happiness will demand satisfaction on all fronts. If an individual happens not to be particularly contemplative, then he may find his happiness nonetheless in the practical life (the life according to virtue), and that happiness will be quite real. But the fully developed human being will have a contemplative side, and he, therefore, besides needing to satisfy his physical desires and to live according to virtue, will only find his complete happiness with the additional satisfaction of the contemplative side of his nature. This happiness is no more real or more true, but it is preferable for men, if they can attain it, because it is the happiness of the more fully developed human.

> For man the best and most pleasant life is the life of the intellect, since the intellect is in the fullest sense the man. So this life will also be the happiest. But life in conformity with the other kind of virtue will be happy in a secondary degree, because activities in accordance with it are human. [1178 a 5]

Note that 'happiness in a secondary degree' implies not less real happiness, but inferior happiness or happiness realised through the baser parts of human nature. There is no inconsistency here therefore, and, if the view is to be challenged, it is to the typically Greek view of human nature, with intellect the prize part, that we should address ourselves rather than the question of happiness itself. The question that needs to be asked is whether 'the intellect *is* in the fullest sense the man'.

2.8 The final preliminary is to point out that, throughout, Aristotle is at great pains to qualify whatever he says is necessary to happiness with the phrase 'in a complete life'. Thus happiness is described as an activity of the soul in accordance with virtue, 'but we must add in a complete life. One swallow does not make a summer; neither does one day. Similarly neither can one day, or a brief space of time, make a man blessed and happy' (1098 a 16). Elsewhere too he stresses that to be called happy one must meet the other conditions involved 'not for some chance period but for a complete life' (1101 a 5).

On the face of it this is quite straightforward. Aristotle appears to be doing no more than taking account of a piece of standard Greek folk wisdom (enshrined in verses such as those of Solon, which he quotes, to the effect that we should call no man happy until he is dead), just as his view that virtuous behaviour lies in the mean between extremes is closely related to the traditional Greek folk maxim 'Nothing in Excess'. And the obvious interpretation of Solon's warning, echoed very clearly in Herodotus,[9] is that it is unwise in the extreme to pronounce on anybody's life until it is over, since even the most blessed of men may suddenly be laid low by disaster. Aristotle therefore may be supposed to be saying that if we are concerned with a happy life (or, better, with a man's happiness through life), we must remember to take his whole life into account, since a moment of disaster can turn his previous happiness to so much dust and ashes.

However this has not stopped commentators reading rather more into the matter, one even arguing that Aristotle is right to claim that there is happiness after death.[10] It is true that Aristotle himself makes heavy weather of Solon's injunction to 'look to the end', wondering if a man can really be happy after his death and perplexed at the notion of the man who having died completely happy constantly changes his mood as a result of swings in fortune for his descendants. But three things should be borne in mind. First, at this juncture Aristotle is toying with various conceivable interpretations of Solon's aphorism, and one of the main conclusions he draws from the present passage is the sensible one that happiness is not simply to be identified with good fortune. Secondly, he writes with the unquestioned premiss that there is an afterlife in which the souls of the dead may experience such human sensations as frustration, pain and happiness. Thirdly, he is well aware of the correct interpretation of Solon even if he does not feel sure that it is correct: for he concedes that Solon's words may mean 'that only when a man is dead can one safely call him blessed as being now beyond the reach of evil misfortune'. Aristotle thinks there is a difficulty in that interpretation because 'it would be strange if ancestors were not affected . . . by the fortunes of their descendants' (1100 a). Few people today will see a continuation of life after death in such human terms, if they believe in one at all. The crucial point is surely that, wherever the truth lies in this matter, Aristotle is confusing a question about the afterlife with a question about happiness, as have certain philosophers since. The question of whether and on what terms the dead can be happy and the question of whether, when a man dies, his life is over, so that we can make a final summing up, are essentially questions about the nature of death.

Finally on this point attention should be drawn to Solomon who argues that we should distinguish between personal and transient desires. The former are the normal type of desire we have, satisfaction of which depends upon our being there; the latter can be satisfied without our physical presence, as for example my desire that my son should be healthy, wealthy and successful may be satisfied in my absence. In so far, he concludes, as my happiness depends upon transient desires 'I cannot truly be called happy until perhaps years after my death' (p.193). There is no doubt, as I have indicated, that at one juncture Aristotle says something very like that, though he seems to be thinking more of calling people fully blessed than of the experience of happiness alone – a distinction that Solomon explicitly rejects for the purpose of his argument. But the fact remains that the sense in which it would be true to say that I cannot be called happy until years after my death seems almost wholly uninteresting. It amounts to saying that, if there is an afterlife in which people are still essentially human and remain aware of events on this earth, they will be satisfied when long-held desires are fulfilled and will not be satisfied in respect of those desires before that time. This is telling us absolutely nothing about what it is for a man to be happy, whether in this life, a life hereafter or both, or about what may contingently bring us happiness. The truth of the matter is as simple as this: generally when we refer to happy people, we mean people disposed to be happy over a period of time. Since it is the case that a happy person might be struck miserable at the age of thirty and remain that way until his death, it is wisest not to insist that a man is a happy man until his life is over. A person should not necessarily be described as a happy person just because he experiences happiness at a particular time and place. A miserable person might experience a moment of happiness. One swallow does not make a summer.

2.9 As we shall see, the problems raised by a reading of Aristotle recur throughout the literature on happiness, none more so than that caused by his failure to differentiate between analysis of and comment about, or on the causes of, happiness. For lurking here are the seeds of such views as that happiness and moral goodness are logically connected, so that a bad man could no more be happy than a bachelor could be married. Yet there is evidently all the difference in the world between saying that as a matter of fact men need friends to be happy and saying that friends are logically necessary and it is therefore logically impossible to be happy without them. The claim that a degree of material prosperity is important for most people's happiness is not the same as the claim that being happy means, in part, being moderately prosperous. Moderation in all things may be wise counsel, but is it the only way to happiness? Perhaps the man who is contemplative by nature thereby experiences happiness of a relatively enduring and self-sufficient sort, but is that to say that his is a more real form of happiness or a greater degree of happiness? Does the fact that man is a conscious being who acts mean that his happiness must be bound up with action? Indeed, does the fact that man is a rational animal mean that his happiness cannot be equated with the contentment of non-rational animals?

Such are some of the distinctions that need to be borne in mind and some of the questions that need to be answered; we are indebted to Aristotle for indirectly having drawn them to our attention.

CHAPTER 3

Some Literary Aphorisms

3.1 There has been a noticeable increase lately in the number of books of quotations, aphorisms and such-like produced. No doubt there are some who would interpret this preoccupation with 'sayings of the week' as a sign of decline in our mental activity. Quoteable quotes rapidly become catch-phrases and catch-phrases are not so far from clichés, about which Eric Partridge recently had this to say:

> a cliché is a stereotyped expression . . . an outworn commonplace . . . a phrase, or short sentence, that has become so hackneyed that careful speakers . . . shrink from it because they feel that its use is an insult to the intelligence of their audience.[1]

I have no doubt that very often, perhaps usually, the use of proverbs, short quotations, aphorisms, tags and other kinds of cliché indicates laziness and 'a half-education – that snare of the half-baked and the ready-made', as Partridge has it, on the part of the speaker. (Though when the clichés include such lines as 'timeo Danaos et dona ferentes', as Partridge's dictionary does, I am inclined to marvel at the quality of a half-education of the past.) Nonetheless that is a point about our use of memorable lines and phrases as a substitute for thought, and not a point about the sayings or quotations themselves. Very often clichés and quoteable quotes have considerable merit in themselves. That indeed is why they are what they are – for they put things well. They often embody metaphors the vivacity of which takes a long time to dull; they may invoke truly illuminating analogies; they may possess the merit of succinctness, of wit, of suggestion, of evocation, of humour or of memorability. In short I have a soft spot for the cliché. And one thing that collections of bon mots, witty sayings or quotations can do, besides entertain, is provide a rough and ready guide to the pulse of a nation – its stock of commonplaces and typical assumptions. That is my excuse for this brief chapter, in which, eschewing the recherché and remarkable, I intend to draw attention to some of the main and enduring ideas about happiness in the Western tradition, through some reasonably well-known references and literary quotations.

3.2 But first attention must be drawn to a possible misuse of literary sources and a danger inherent in contemporary philosophy. Much modern philosophy, avowedly concerned with conceptual analysis, which is to say trying to determine what makes something what it is or what constitutes an instance of it, relies on the ordinary day-to-day use of language and approaches a given concept by asking what sort of thing the plain man in the street would normally say using the word in question. Thus, in trying to determine what justice is or what makes an act just, one might consider whether one would ever say something such as 'That's just; it really hurt him'; or we might ask what we would say if confronted by a case of a particular kind – would we call it 'just' or would we not? There are evidently limitations to this approach, and dangers if the limits are not observed. There are initial problems such as the questions of who the plain man is and who decides what he would say in hypothetical situations – but none so great as the question of whether what he would say is actually of any importance. Clearly the fact that we would regard it as unintelligible for someone to maintain that 'John is a bachelor and married' is important. But it is not clear that the fact that people in general might not think it makes sense to say 'he is a member of the National Front and a just man' tells us any more than that people in general don't *think* that the National Front has just views, which is not the same thing as saying that it does not and cannot. The basic point here is that pointing to the fact that somebody or some set of people regard a remark as meaningful is not sufficient to show that it is.

When use is made of literature or literary examples in philosophy, there is a danger of committing this error (of treating what is thought to be intelligible as synonymous with what is intelligible) at one remove – of taking what a fictional character is made to say as evidence of intelligibility. This error may take the form either of quoting a fictional character's remarks on the presumption that they are meaningful or of quoting his views on what is meaningful. It *may,* of course, be perfectly permissible to cite fictional characters either as examples of language users or for their stated opinions, provided that the fact that they exhibit or lay claim to some view is not regarded either as evidence that the plain man would do likewise or as evidence that we should. Obviously the fact that a fictional character is made to say something does not necessarily mean that a real person would say it: the author may be satirising him, depicting him as an imbecile or revealing his own imbecility. But even if the character is presumed to be normal, strictly speaking that tells us only that, as things are, it seems to some of us to make sense to make the claim in question.

Thus, it is quite reasonable that Robert Dearden should refer to a character in Albert Camus' novel *The Plague* in order to illustrate a point of his own.[2] The old Spaniard in the novel is allegedly happy spending his life in bed transferring dried peas from one saucepan to another. Dearden's point is that, to some of us at least, such a way of finding happiness seems unintelligible. Similarly, and again quite legitimately, in raising the question of whether a deluded person should be regarded as happy he cites the character Hialmar Ekdal from Ibsen's *Wild Duck* as a case in point. As he says 'the play is an exploration of the clash which can occur between happiness and truth' (p.25). Provided he is not suggesting that it proves that the deluded person is not happy, all is well. It would not be well if he thought that this was evidence for his view; at best it is evidence that somebody shares it.

However, in a subsequent paper, he does seem to think that in citing fictional characters he is proving something about the happiness they happen to be talking about.[3] That is quite different and quite illegitimate. This time he quotes Nora's statement from the third act of Ibsen's *A Doll's House*: 'I thought I was [happy]; but I never was'. That is treated as evidence that objective judgements about whether people are happy or not make sense, whereas in fact it shows only that the fictional character Nora is made to express the belief (implicitly) that they do. In the same paper Dearden goes on to make the same kind of mistake twice more, referring to Aldous Huxley's *Brave New World* and C.P. Snow's *The Masters.* But reading about characters who *believe* they face a conflict of values (as in the latter book) does not establish that such perceptions are adequate; it constitutes no argument in favour of a pluralistic theory of value, as Dearden would have it.

Illuminating or illustrative references to literature in respect of happiness are not uncommon amongst philosophers. Theodore Benditt quotes an exchange between Creon and Antigone from Anouilh's *Antigone* to illustrate two different conceptions of happiness (the Epicurean and the Aristotelian) which is quite legitimate,[4] just as it is legitimate for Hallet to quote Johnson's assertion that all happy people are not necessarily equally happy, as a point of view.[5] In exactly the same way, and equally reasonably and effectively, one might throw passages into a debate about happiness from a superficially rather more unlikely source such as Agatha Christie:

> 'He's just one of the usual unhappy successes.'
> 'Unhappy?'
> 'Most successes are unhappy. That's why they are successes — they have to reassure themselves by achieving something that the world will notice.'
> 'What extraordinary ideas you have, Anthony.'[6]

Whether Anthony's ideas are or are not extraordinary is neither here nor there. The point is that we have here a view about happiness, rather than a turn of phrase involving the word happiness, and we use it as a source rather than a proof.

On the other hand, Rescher, who quotes Butler in a footnote, seems to verge on the illegitimate. Butler writes in *The Way of All Flesh*:

> It is hard enough to know whether one is happy or unhappy now, and still harder to compare the relative happiness or unhappiness of different times of one's life; the utmost that can be said is that we are fairly happy so long as we are not distinctly aware of being miserable.

That is a point of view: the view that judgements involving comparison between present and past happiness — even one's own — are 'notoriously problematic'.[7] It is not evidence for that view; quoting Butler adds nothing to Rescher's case (except weight of opinion). Both Butler and Rescher might simply misunderstand the nature of happiness and be mistaken in their view.

Nor, incidentally, is this mistaken technique of treating written statements as evidence or proof rather than data confined to discussions of happiness. To cite but one example from a quite different topic, Randall, in his paper 'The "really" real', bases his whole inquiry on a passage from a review of a book of poems, which contains the remark 'No one will expect the life-blood of realism in a book which blazons on its first page "Dedicated to Reality" ', as if, since somebody wrote it, the remark must be meaningful and throw light on the nature of reality.[8] (For all I know it may be and do so. But there is no reason to suppose that it necessarily *must.*) Taken to its extreme this approach leads to the position of philosophers such as J.L. Austin, so ably criticised by Ernest Gellner and more recently Keith Graham, which involves bypassing the traditional philosophical problem of reality (which is essentially whether there is any reality beyond a world of appearances) because ordinary folk don't use the word 'real' in ways that betray any sense of this as a real problem. As we shall see below, something of the same limitation attaches to other philosophers, besides Dearden, considering the concept of happiness.[9]

3.3 Under the heading of the literary background two strands may be picked out: fiction and popular non-fiction. Fiction's preoccupation with happiness, as something either to be examined through or by its characters or to be sought by or wished upon them, must be evident to the most casual of readers. No need, therefore, to emphasise that books as diverse as Tolstoy's *War and Peace,* Iris Murdoch's *The Black Prince* and Henry James' *Portrait of a Lady* are all centrally, if not exclusively, about man's search for happiness. Nor would it be profitable to seek to catalogue all significant references to happiness in literature. Instead I shall content myself with offering examples of some of the main ideas, themes and views to have had a long history in Western literature.

The literature of the classical world (not always easy to categorise, but seldom strictly speaking fiction as we know it) harps on a few well-worn and by now familiar themes: Aristotle's view that happiness and virtue are closely connected is often echoed — thus Archytas claims that the wicked man must always be unhappy,[10] while both Seneca and Cicero state that true happiness is centred in virtue.[11] 'No one', says the former, 'can be called happy who is living a life of falsehood.'[12] Archytas and Cicero both follow Aristotle also in recognising that there is an element of fortune in the experience of happiness, although Cicero is careful to add that 'happiness consists in good fortune allied to good design',[13] thereby stressing yet a third

Aristotelian strand: the link between happiness and reason. Seneca devotes some attention to this point in a letter on the subject of happiness: 'The happy life depends upon this and this alone: our attainment of perfect reason,'[14] because, he argues, reason can be used to buck one's spirits up when they are down. Apart from the stress on reason, virtue and fortune, and odd comments such as that old age and happiness are seldom found together, the bulk of classical literature dwells upon man's uncomfortable lot and thinks in terms of resignation rather than joy, following on, in fact, from Solon's cry that 'No mortal is born happy, all are wretched upon whom the sun looks down'. This is echoed by Theognis, Sophocles and Euripides several times.[15] 'No happiness can mortals call their own', writes Euripides, 'for the Gods can always wipe it out.'[16] Several hundred years later the same pessimism is to be found in the otherwise very different poetry of Ovid: 'None can we call happy until his corpse is laid in the tomb.'[17] Given the prevalence of a gloomy outlook, and indeed a rough life, it is not surprising perhaps that Seneca sees the happy life in terms of 'security and perpetual tranquility',[18] or that Juvenal while paying lip-service (tongue in cheek?) to the power of reason should add 'they too are to be deemed happy who have learnt under the schooling of life to endure its ills without fretting against the yoke'.[19]

3.4 One of the most interesting things about the treatment of happiness in the subsequent literature of the English speaking world (to which I shall now arbitrarily confine myself for the most part) is the way in which, despite close affinities with the classical world, it almost entirely turns its back upon the assumption that virtue and reason go hand in hand with happiness. In fact, in some of the most searching literature concerned with this topic, such as Joseph Conrad's fiction, the very reverse seems to be implied. Knowledge, particularly self-knowledge, is seen as a potent source of suffering and despair, and in a sophisticated way the 'angel-infancy' referred to by Henry Vaughan,[20] the simple innocence that allows of happiness, is contrasted with the tortured soul of a Hamlet that can gain no peace. The proverb 'Better to be happy than wise' was noted as early as Heywood's Dictionary of 1546, and these famous lines from Gray make the point even more explicitly:

Since sorrow never comes too late
And happiness too swiftly flies
Thought would destroy their paradise.
No more. Where ignorance is bliss
Tis folly to be wise.[21]

It is only a short step from that view to the idea of the rustic life of the peasant being the source of true happiness: 'Oh God, methinks it were a happy life to be no better than a homely swain.'[22]

The view that happiness is the special province of the simple man leads on to a variety of closely related themes: there is a nostalgic longing for the country life that goes back at least as far as the Roman poet Horace and that asserts that true happiness can only be found away from the city, playing on the familiar stereotypical contrast between innocent rustic and sophisticated townsman. 'Happy the man whose wish and care a few paternal acres bound, content to breathe his native air on his own ground.'[23] Sometimes the idea is carried to the point of claiming that what the head doesn't know the heart can't grieve over, as when Othello cries 'I had been happy, if the general camp, Pioners and all, had tasted her sweet body, so had I nothing known'.[24] Very marked indeed is another attitude that survives from the classical viewpoint, namely resignation to one's lot as essential for happiness. Thus Bernard Shaw suggests that in order to be happy as a servant one needs to have the soul of a servant,[25] while Erasmus states simply that 'it is the chiefest point of happiness that a man is willing to be what he is'.[26] And this in turn relates to one of the commonest themes of all: the way to happiness lies in *not* searching for it. Aldous Huxley compares it to coke — 'something you get as a by-product in the process of making something else';[27] there are innumerable quips along the lines of William Feather's 'Some of us might find happiness if we would quit struggling so desperately for it';[28] John Stuart Mill in his autobiography remarked that one ceases to be happy so soon as one asks oneself whether one is, and the Marquis de Vauvenargues suggests that 'there are men who are happy without knowing it', though, on the face of it at least, that would seem far fetched.[29] Less contentious and perhaps wiser and more illuminating is Montesquieu's suggestion that 'if we only wanted to be happy, it would be easy; but we want to be happier than other people, which is almost always difficult, since we think them happier than they are'.[30] But it is a chance remark of Edward de Bono's that seems to me to get nearest the mark and that comes close to the view of happiness for which I shall argue in the second part of this book: 'Unhappiness is best defined as the difference between our talents and our expectations.'[31]

3.5 'Who is the happy warrior?'[32] Wordsworth's answer to his own question encompasses most of the above ideas, though he retains also something of the classical view that moral stature and reason come into the picture. The happy warrior is he 'who, doomed to go in company with pain, and fear and bloodshed, miserable train, turns his necessity to glorious gain'. He controls his passions, accepts reason as his law, keeps his trust, eschews worldly ambition and fame, and yet can rise to meet the highest call of duty. But most of all he is one who remains steadfast of purpose in the face of all changes of fortune. That is true too of the happy man depicted by Wotton in his poem 'The Character of a Happy Life'. But Wotton emphasises rather more than Wordsworth the independence that the happy man has from various wants, fears and aspirations (envy, ambition, passion, pride) that might stand in his way:

> This man is freed from servile bands
> Of hope to rise, or fear to fall;
> Lord of himself, though not of lands;
> And having nothing, yet hath all.[33]

In much the same spirit Thomas Dekker had written:

> Art thou poor, yet hath thou golden slumbers?
> O sweet content. Art thou rich, yet in thy mind perplexed?
> O punishment.[34]

These views very obviously reflect those of Plato, according to whom justice, wisdom and happiness are closely interrelated. He envisages a soul in man that has three parts, that of reason, that of will-power and that of spontaneous desire. Those individuals who are capable of living their lives as the rational part of them determines, so that their desires are rationally ordered and controlled and their will-power is allied with reason, besides being wise and just, will experience true happiness.

Dekker refers to 'content' and here as elsewhere the question arises as to whether happiness, satisfaction, content, pleasure and so on are more or less synonymous terms. Opinions differ. Dryden's view that 'all the happiness mankind can gain is not in pleasure, but in rest from pain' implies that, call it what you will, men cannot gain true happiness, but only something inferior that might be referred to as relief, tranquillity, peace or possibly contentment.[35] Johnson suggests that 'a peasant and a philosopher may be equally satisfied, but not equally happy. Happiness consists in the multiplicity of agreeable consciousness', a view that many might share, though very often for different reasons.[36] Tolstoy introduces a different emphasis with his view that happiness consists in the 'satisfaction of the daily needs of existence'.[37]

What is less, if at all, disputed is the value of happiness. Shaw, admittedly, makes a character exclaim that no man could bear a lifetime of happiness.[38] But Pope's celebrated lines represent the usual view:

> O happiness our being's end and aim
> Good pleasure, ease, content, whate'er thy name
> That something still which prompts the eternal sigh
> For which we bear to live or dare to die.[39]

More bluntly Richard Cambridge asks (in advance of the systematical philosophy of utilitarianism, though not of Francis Hutcheson who was the first to talk of the greatest happiness of the greatest number[40]) 'What is the worth of anything but for the happiness twill bring?'[41]

3.6 There are besides a number of isolated, scattered, sometimes contradictory suggestions to be found in various literary nooks and crannies. 'What happiness to reign a lonely king?' wonders Tennyson, raising both the question of the relationship between wealth and happiness and that between companionship and happiness.[42] Milton has Adam and God engaged in a long dialogue on the latter issue, it being finally agreed that the answer to the question 'in solitude what happiness?' is not very much for Adam, though the case is allowed to be different with God.[43] But perhaps that view should be qualified by Ben Jonson's suggestion that 'true happiness consists not in the multitude of friends, but in the worth and choice'.[44] On the first of the two points raised by Tennyson, there has always been widespread agreement that great wealth is not necessary for happiness and cannot guarantee it. There has been less unanimity on whether *some* wealth is necessary and whether wealth alone *could* bring happiness. Finally the question of whether marriage can ever be a truly happy state seems to be of perennial interest!

Overall the literary background gives an abiding impression that happiness is a central concern of mankind, while a widespread sense of melancholy, often giving way to frustration, aimlessness and despair, is mankind's common experience. Typically happiness seems to be conceived not in terms of any particular goods so much as in terms of being in harmony with one's lot, but Samuel Butler adds a most interesting thought to any straightforward conception of happiness: 'Happiness and misery consist in a progression towards better or worse; it does not matter how high up or low down you are, it depends not on this, but on the direction in which you are tending.'[45]

3.7 Popular non-fiction on the subject of happiness generally consists of nostrums: clichés dressed up as profound truths and strategies for acquiring happiness, of the type 'make friends' — easier to recognise the need for than to do. I do not intend to extend the same courtesy to this branch of literature as I have to others by reviewing it. But one such book should perhaps be singled out and summarised, and that is Bertrand Russell's *The Conquest of Happiness.*[46] This book neither involves nor displays the erudition for which Russell was justly famed. It is not sound philosophy, great philosopher though Russell no doubt was. It is however of sufficient appeal and interest to merit attention.

His avowed purpose is to suggest, not so much ways of ameliorating social conditions, but rather 'a cure for the ordinary day-to-day unhappiness from which most people in civilised countries suffer' (p. 13). To that end the first half of the book is devoted to locating some of the key causes of unhappiness — the result being a somewhat random mixture of psychological, logical and contingent claims of varying interest and plausibility. One major premiss is that self-absorbtion of various kinds is a most common cause (or source — Russell does not distinguish the two clearly) of unhappiness, and, he suggests, such self-absorbtion is often the result of childhood deprivation of some sort or another. Russell is captivated by a particular view of human nature such that he cannot accept that man could find happiness in the absence of any challenge. Man needs a struggle: 'the mere absence of effort from his life removes an essential ingredient of happiness' (p. 23). It is true that he also remarks that 'a happy life must be to a great extent a quiet life, for it is only in an atmosphere of quiet that true joy can live' (p. 52), and also that he sees an emphasis on competitive success as 'the main source of happiness' as misplaced (p. 39). But those are qualifications to his fundamental belief that true happiness is to be found in the thrill of the chase – a view that elsewhere leads him to deny that apparent contentment in totalitarian states can constitute real happiness.[47]

He sees fatigue caused by worry as detrimental to happiness, though here, as so often, it is unclear whether the claim is that happiness is by definition the kind of thing that is incompatible with worry or something that as a matter of fact tends to get displaced by worries. He denies that things like drink can bring true happiness: 'Drunkeness is temporary suicide; the happiness that it brings is merely negative, a momentary cessation of unhappiness' (p. 19). Here we have an echo of Dryden amongst others and an intimation of a distinction between happiness and an absence of unhappiness that we shall meet in the philosophical literature.

The role of reason in happiness also receives attention. 'Most men and women are very deficient in control over their thoughts' (p. 55). Russell explains that by that he means that they cannot cease to think about worrying matters, even when it is profitless to go on thinking about them. In other ways too they fail to be as rational as they might: envy leads to unhappiness, but we do not have to be passive victims of envy. It is possible to some extent to control one's emotions: 'merely to realise the causes of one's own envious feelings is to take a large step towards curing them' (p. 67). This line of thought leads Russell to assert that our happiness could be increased 'by the cultivation of an orderly mind' (p. 56) or that mental discipline is a cure for unhappiness. By reason we may control our emotions, overcome our prejudices (such as a sense of sin), have the wit to avoid comparing ourselves with others and in other similar ways keep better control over our happiness.

The first half of the book ends with the reassertion of the positive view that 'the happiness that is genuinely satisfying is accompanied by the fullest exercise of our faculties and the fullest realisation of the world in which we live' (p. 85), and the superficially rather curious assertion that 'to almost everybody sympathetic surroundings are necessary to happiness' (p. 99). Could there be *anyone,* we shall have to ask below, to whom they would not be necessary? Is not the remark practically a tautology?

3.8 The second half of the book concentrates on causes of happiness. Russell begins by making a distinction between what he calls animal happiness, which is possible for any human being, and spiritual happiness, which is possible 'only to those who can read and write' (p. 111). Such a distinction raises the question of whether both types of happiness are true happiness, equally happy, equally valuable and so forth. Russell avoids these questions, remarking only in passing that 'the difference made by education is only in regard to the activities by which [happiness can be] obtained' (p. 112).

His positive prescriptions include the recommendation that we should adopt 'an expansive and generous attitude towards other people' (p. 82), have wide interests, be friendly in attitude. Rather more interesting is his reference to the importance of a feeling of security and modest self-confidence. A degree of modesty, he suggests, brings its own reward: 'the man who underestimates himself is perpetually being surprised by success' (p. 113). Nonetheless, some sense of one's own value in the judgement of others is essential, and he concludes that, if it is true that (at the time of writing) men of science were more happy than others, the reason was that 'in their work they are happy because the importance [of science] is not doubted either by themselves or laymen . . . When the public cannot understand a picture or a poem, they conclude that it is a bad picture or a bad poem. When they cannot understand the theory of relativity they [conclude] rightly that their education has been insufficient'. (p. 113) The idea that self-esteem and security are crucial to happiness recurs both explicitly ('those who face life with a feeling of security are much happier than those who face it with a feeling of insecurity, at any rate so long as their sense of security does not lead them to disaster' – p. 113) and implicitly in Russell's reflection on the increasing failure of family life to provide happiness and the need for the individual to have pride in his work.

Russell's conclusion is that personal happiness 'depends partly upon external circumstances and partly on oneself' (p. 186). The former should include a modicum of prosperity, some degree of challenge and scope for altering one's lot ('opportunities for ambition') and some reason for pride and the exercise of skill in one's work. The latter should involve continuity of purpose ('one of the most essential ingredients of happiness in the long run') and both resignation and effort: resignation in the face of implacable circumstance; effort to make one's world as one would like it to be. Such a view sees a role for education in respect of happiness: 'It should be our endeavour therefore, both in education and in attempts to adjust ourselves to the world, to aim at avoiding self-centred passions and at acquiring those affections and those interests which will prevent our thoughts from dwelling perpetually on ourselves' (p. 187).

3.9 I have included this brief resumé of Russell's *Conquest of Happiness* in this chapter rather than elsewhere because it shares with the other literary background material an absence of argument, reasoning or evidence to support its contentions.[48] The material in this chapter has all been essentially speculative. That does not of course mean that it is necessarily false or foolish, and I shall take up some of the ideas introduced here in subsequent chapters.

There are many other speculative assertions that might be quoted, ranging down the Beatles' song lyric 'happiness is a warm gun', through the advertisement claiming that 'happiness is a cigar called Hamlet' or that 'happiness is receiving a phone call from someone you love', by way of the view that real happiness is to be found in books, forward to the suggestion of theorists such as Erich Fromm that security is essential to happiness, in and out of the backwaters of Freudian assertions about sexual guilt, along the path of religious revivalism, until we end up heaven knows where. But now that we have at any rate a broad picture of the literary man's opinions through the ages, if not the man in the street's, it is time to turn our attention to more systematic attempts to make sense of these and other claims—to leave behind the question of what some people *happen* to have said about happiness and consider what some have argued can *truly* be said of happiness.

CHAPTER 4

The Philosophical Tradition

4.1 Intellectual interest in happiness, and how and whether to seek it, did not die with Aristotle. The next person to base his philosophy of life on the notion was Epicurus, a Greek who set up his school in Athens during the third century BC. It was Epicurus who first countered Aristotle by claiming that man *could* be happy even on the rack. He maintains that pleasure is 'the beginning and end of a happy life' but, again parting company with Aristotle, he stresses the importance of static as opposed to dynamic pleasures, that is to say those pleasures that are the outcome of an absence of desire rather than the gratification of a desire: the sort of pleasure that arises out of avoiding hunger, frustration, or thirst, rather than the satisfaction of lust, gluttony or debauchery. He counsels the pursuit of equilibrium rather than ecstasy, and emphasises the absence of pain rather than the presence of joy. In this contrast with Aristotle we get the beginnings of a distinction (noted in the previous chapter) that some would like to draw between happiness, properly understood, and mere contentment.

It is the particular sense that Epicurus gives to happiness that allows the unwary to regard his philosophy as similar to stoicism, despite the fact that the two are essentially dissimilar. The founding father of the stoic philosophy is usually taken to have been Zeno, who was a contemporary of Epicurus and likewise settled in Athens; but later adherents to the continually developing philosophy included Seneca, adviser to the Roman Emperor Nero (by whom he was subsequently required to commit suicide), Epictetus, originally a slave but subsequently one of Nero's right-hand men, and one of the Emperors themselves: Marcus Aurelius. The essence of stoicism actually involves the rejection of happiness as a worthy end, along with such worldly goods as wealth, fame and health; in its place virtue is seen as the only proper objective in life: virtue of and for its own sake. But, at least as popularly understood and as revealed in the life of men like Seneca, what this meant in practice was the cultivation of a calm and unruffled countenance in the face of the calamities of daily life. Believing that external circumstances such as poverty, disease or indeed an order to commit suicide ought not to upset the individual's capacity to live virtuously, the stoics were inevitably led to a belief in the power of mind over matter. Everything of real importance was under the control of individual will. Hence the actual goal of stoicism became again a kind of equilibrium that the individual could maintain in spite of outward misfortune. It is this that superficially resembles the equilibrium pursued by Epicurus, as one can see from this remark of Epictetus: 'Athens is beautiful. Yes, but happiness is far more beautiful – happiness, that is to say freedom from passion and disturbance, the sense that your affairs depend on noone.'[1]

Several centuries later something of the stoic spirit, if not the stoic philosophy, remains in the work of Boethius. Outward fortune did not smile on him: he was imprisoned and executed by Theodoric, the king of Italy, whom he had apparently served faithfully. In the *Consolation of Philosophy,* written while in prison, Boethius too argues for the goodness of happiness. But it is clear that in his work happiness is more akin to a state of blessedness ('Men are made happy by the obtaining of divinity') than to either pleasure or resignation, despite the stoic endurance he displayed in life.[2]

In the seventeenth century Thomas Hobbes, despite his fundamentally gloomy view of human nature, and though he said little about happiness or, to use his term, felicity, nonetheless made at least one important observation: 'Felicity . . . by which we mean continual delight, consisteth not in having prospered, but in prospering.'[3] Implicit in this is the view that happiness is not strictly speaking an end comparable to fame or wealth, which a man can pursue and perhaps acquire, but is rather something supervenient on the successful attainment of other ends. With John Locke we find the stirrings of a psychological hedonism, that is to say the view that man by nature cannot but pursue his happiness, which was later to gain prominence as being, supposedly, an important aspect of the utilitarian philosophy. Locke appears to have believed that fundamentally everyone must always be moved solely by desire for his own happiness. 'What is it moves desire? . . . I answer happiness and that alone.' Furthermore he asserts, anticipating a quite different aspect of utilitarianism, 'things are good or bad only in relation to pleasure or pain'.[4] It is only as a result of that firm conviction that Locke comes to the conclusion that liberty is much to be prized; for he argues that in the long run the individual's self-interest coincides with the general interest, and that therefore a situation in which people are free to pursue their self-interest will lead to the satisfaction of the general interest. It is interesting to contrast that view of the nature of the connection between freedom and happiness with the currently more fashionable one that true happiness depends upon freedom (a view held, for instance, by Russell). In his notebooks, during 1668, Locke put down the emphatic statement that 'It is man's proper business to seek happiness and avoid misery'. Happiness, he explains, 'consists in what delights and contents the mind; misery in what disturbs, discomposes or torments it'. He then proceeds to enumerate five pleasures that are particularly lasting (or as we might prefer to put it five long-lasting and secure sources of pleasure): health, reputation, knowledge, doing good and contemplation of an afterlife. By rationally pursuing these and refusing to be tempted by immediate but short-lived and possibly even ultimately damaging pleasures, Locke suggests he may be master of his own happiness.

Not all philosophers, of course, have been equally impressed or indeed impressed at all by the claims of happiness. Kant's moral philosophy, with its emphasis on being virtuous for its own sake, which has more than a touch of the stoic about it, pays scant attention to the value of happiness. Schopenhauer's gloomy outlook saw only a choice between the affliction of unsatisfied desires or the boredom of satiety. To that dilemma he offered the even less attractive solution of the subjugation of the will, through chastity, poverty, fasting and so on, whereby a state of nothingness might be achieved – one hardly dares say 'enjoyed'. Nonetheless the history of philosophy as a whole shows a marked concern for happiness. That concern increased with the advent and widespread appeal of utilitarianism during the nineteenth century.

4.2 As a matter of fact the utilitarians did not always use the word 'happiness', and when they did they did not pause to offer very searching or thorough accounts of what they took it to be. Jeremy

Bentham, the most effective father of utilitarianism though not the originator of the essential doctrine, merely echoes Locke when he asserts that mankind has been placed under the guidance of two sovereign masters: pleasure and pain.[5] John Stuart Mill, to whom subsequent utilitarianism owes something of its sophistication, embroiders on that terminology only to the extent of saying that he understands by happiness 'pleasure and the absence of pain; by unhappiness pain and the privation of pleasure'.[6] Nonetheless it is clear that happiness was regarded as the supreme value in the utilitarian ethic so that 'actions are right in proportion as they tend to promote happiness, wrong as they tend to produce the reverse of happiness'.[7] The real advance here over the previous centuries of talk about happiness is the explicit avowal that the pursuit of happiness is not just a natural tendency or an understandable predilection, but a moral duty.

If Aristotle's *Ethics* gives rise to most of the conceptual questions about happiness, the work of Bentham and Mill gives rise to most of the questions surrounding the value of happiness. Inevitably, therefore, the problems in their work have dominated subsequent discussion. Is happiness the supreme moral end? Do men necessarily pursue it? Is the injunction to pursue the greatest happiness of the greatest number coherent and plausible? In addition there has been a split between act and rule utilitarians, the former arguing that each individual action should be assessed by the utilitarian criterion of maximising happiness, the latter that certain rules of conduct should be formulated by reference to that criterion and thereafter followed as the moral law. There have been attempts to rewrite utilitarianism, while retaining something of its essential spirit, around some value such as human welfare rather than happiness. Narveson has gone so far as to argue that what the supreme value of utilitarianism is called is unimportant: the essential point is that the values that people do as a matter of fact hold (the desires they actually have; the states of affairs they want realised) should provide the yardstick for a system of moral values.[8] In other words he interprets utilitarianism as investing people's overall wants with ethical significance. Such an account of utilitarianism does draw attention to its strength as a theory that can be built on the ruins of all other ethical theories; but it also betrays its possible weakness as an innately conservative theory, a point taken up by MacIntyre in his paper 'Against utilitarianism'.[9]

4.3 In 1963 Von Wright's book, *The Varieties of Goodness,* was published.[10] That influential book will serve as a useful beginning to a brief survey of the most recent developments in the philosophical literature concerning happiness, which, in turn, will help to pinpoint some of the issues that have to be resolved before we can revert to the empirical evidence and draw some conclusions about happiness and schooling.

Von Wright distinguishes between three ideals of happiness that we have already encountered: the Aristotelian view that happiness is to be found in action, the Epicurean ideal according to which ' "true happiness" derives above all from *having* things which please' ('things', incidentally, being interpreted widely to include things like agreeable memories as well as things like nice homes), and the utilitarian ideal, which sees happiness as something akin to contentment: 'an equilibrium between needs and wants on the one hand and satisfaction on the other' (p. 93). He adds, as a subspecies of the last, the ascetic ideal wherein the desired equilibrium is achieved by setting oneself a low threshold of need or a limited range of wants. However, he rapidly dismisses this as a crippled and mistaken view. Asceticism, he claims, may prevent unhappiness, but unhappiness is a contrary not a contradictory of happiness. In other words it may be conceded that having minimal wants may lead to minimal frustration, which means in turn minimal unhappiness. But minimal unhappiness does not mean maximum happiness or indeed happiness at all. We shall return to this point below (5.14).

Apart from his rejection of the ascetic, Von Wright does not make much effort to adjudicate between the ideals he introduces. He confines himself to observing that the notion that happiness is to be found through passive pleasures such as those of possession, though possibly risky in practice, is not logically odd. What he brings out well in his subsequent discussion is the need to distinguish between the conditions that are *as a matter of fact* necessary or suitable to allow people to be happy, and the *defining* characteristics of happiness. With a clarity that Aristotle could have done with, he separates the question of what happiness is from the question of what factors are likely to determine whether someone will experience it. He then further divides the factors in question into three distinct groups: chance factors, dispositional factors and factors depending on human agency. Thus, it may be the case that my happiness over the next decade will be variously affected by factors such as the death of my mother (chance), my bodily health, resilient spirit and limited talents (all dispositional) and the steps I take in the changing circumstances along the way (human agency). Such categorisation will be of some importance when we come to consider the question of our control over happiness (8.6).

He turns next to the question of what is involved in being happy, and suggests that a distinction should be drawn between 'a happy man' and 'a happy life', the latter being of wider scope. The suggestion is probably best resisted, simply because insistence on such usage would prove confusing. But the point that lies behind the suggestion is surely correct: there is a sense in which we can accept that someone is a happy man (generally or by disposition), even while knowing that he is unhappy (at the moment). Certainly some kind of a distinction must be drawn between remarks such as 'The news of the disaster made him unhappy' and remarks such as 'He lived for another twenty years after the death of his wife, but he was an unhappy man'.

Approaching the basic conceptual question about happiness Von Wright asserts that 'to be happy is to be in a certain relationship . . . a relationship to one's circumstances of life . . . Happiness is not in the circumstances . . . but springs into being with the relationship . . To judge oneself happy is to pass judgement on or value one's circumstances of life' (p. 98). Then in rapid succession he provides succinct, if debateable, answers to two crucial questions: can first person judgements and can third person judgements about happiness be mistaken? The answer he gives to the latter question is yes, while admitting that third person remarks of the form 'he is happy' are ambiguous. On the one hand, such a remark may involve disguised prescription; that is to say, in asserting that someone else is happy the speaker may be trying to insist on a particular view of the nature of happiness ('Of course he's happy. He's got a lovely wife and a good job hasn't he?'). On the other hand, more often such remarks are straightforward descriptions that are either true or false, depending on whether the agent referred to does or does not value the relationship to his circumstances in which he finds himself. As to the first person judgement, Von Wright suggests that it should be taken as 'final, whatever we think we should say, if we were in his circumstances' (p. 99). The fact that we would not be happy in a particular set of circumstances, and cannot readily comprehend that anybody else could be, cannot stand against the agent's own judgement that he is happy. The only ways in which Von Wright allows that the first person agent might be mistaken about his own happiness are cases of telling a lie or insincerity. The net result, on this view, is that when it comes to happiness 'the supreme judge of the case must be the subject himself' in the present, although it is conceded that this does not mean that 'every man is the best and most competent judge of his prospects of happiness' (p. 99). That is certainly not the case, and Von Wright's suggestion that it is because we appreciate that we can make mistakes about our future happiness that we often assume we can be mistaken about our present happiness, is plausible.

4.4 An important feature of Von Wright's analysis of happiness is the implication that there are no objective necessary criteria of happiness (the corollary of the view that the agent cannot be mistaken about his own happiness). That view has been challenged by Jean Austin, Anthony Kenny and Richard Hare amongst others. Austin[11] asserts that ascribing happiness to someone is 'the highest assessment of his total condition' and such an appraisal is incompatible with certain things, such as his being 'unkind' or on drugs, while Kenny,[12] by arguing that the martyr who chooses death or the young girl who renounces marriage to nurse a sick mother could not conceivably be pursuing happiness, likewise implicitly sets limits to the terms on which one could properly speaking be said to be happy.

In *Freedom and Reason*[13] Hare does concede that the subject's own view about his happiness or lack of it has to be taken into account. 'However highly we appraise the state of life of a person we cannot call him happy, if he himself hates every minute of his existence' (p. 128). He regards it as a mistake, therefore, to treat happiness statements as 'implying no report on a man's state of mind'. But he thinks it equally mistaken to see them 'as nothing but such a report' (p. 129). He too sees them as essentially appraisals.

> Suppose [he writes] that we ask whether a mental defective is happy . . . suppose he in fact gets all the things which he likes and none of the things that he dislikes . . . Are we supposed to call him happy? . . . although we should admit that in a sense he was happy, we should then say 'look what he's missing' . . . 'he's not

> really happy' or 'he's not happy in the fullest sense of the word.' [p. 127]

It is not altogether clear what Hare means by 'really happy' and 'happy in the fullest sense of the word' as opposed to 'happy'. But it is clear that at the end of the day he will not acknowledge that the mental defective could be happy, and that he sees that as a matter of logic rather than contingent fact. 'Before we call a man happy we find it necessary to be sure, not only that his desires are satisfied, but also that the complete set of his desires is one which we are not very much averse to having ourselves' (p. 128). Superficially there is an ambiguity in the last sentence: Hare might simply mean that we are psychologically indisposed to call a man happy except in such circumstances. But the context makes it clear that he is arguing rather that 'happiness', except on such conditions, wouldn't constitute true happiness.

4.5 Roger Montague in a refreshingly crisp paper takes a quite different view, more in line with Von Wright's account.[14] He argues for three necessary and sufficient conditions of happiness. First, to be happy, the agent must lack any standing dissatisfaction that he regards as serious (a dissatisfaction is explained as involving both not getting what one wants and being aware of that fact). Secondly, happiness involves the achievement of all of at least one's most important goals, which consideration leads Montague to reject the views of those such as Sidgwick that the greatest possible happiness equals the greatest attainable surplus of pleasure over pain. Even if you have a large aggregate of pleasure over pain, you cannot, logically cannot, be happy if certain of your crucial goals remain unachieved. The third condition is located by means of a consideration of the connection between contentment and happiness. Following what he takes to be Mill's view, Montague, noting that one can be 'wildly happy' but not 'wildly contented' and that we can ask 'are you happy, I don't mean merely contented' but not vice versa, concludes that happiness implies something more positive than contentment, which is merely a matter of not being dissatisfied. Thus, he writes, 'on my view having no standing dissatisfactions, achieving goals (subject to qualifications) and being positively pleased about the way things are going make a man happy in a constitutive sense of make' (p. 98).

He rounds off his paper by sketching the areas of agreement that he finds he shares with Aristotle: happiness can be pursued; it is a final end, but can be more choiceworthy with extras such as health or wealth; and it is self-sufficient in the sense that 'the happy man does not want anything further'. It is not however self-sufficient in the sense of irrefragible or inviolate, though possibly he who finds his happiness in the contemplative life may have a relatively secure happiness. Montague dissents from Aristotle on the question of the way in which it makes sense to regard children as happy: 'we call a child happy to indicate its demeanour and not as Aristotle said to express our congratulations and hopes for his eventual successful exercise of his capacity for characteristic human activity' (p. 99). And how may we best set about gaining happiness? As to that, 'novels and real life must be our tutors' (p. 102).

4.6 In a paper published in 1968,[15] John Wilson agrees with Hare that 'a man can say I'm happy and be wrong' on the grounds, different from Hare's, that a man can make mistakes about his mental state and that happiness is not exclusively geared to wants. 'Even in momentary happiness . . . a man may fail to notice or pay attention to how he feels', and he can be mistaken because 'he does not attend closely enough to the evidence' (p. 16). But Wilson nonetheless insists that being and feeling happy go hand in hand. He draws attention to the distinction between being and feeling ill on the one hand, where the two can be divorced, and feeling and being in pain on the other, where they cannot. I can be ill and not feel ill; I can feel ill and not be ill. But, if I feel pain, I am in pain, even if its putative cause is illusory, and if I am in pain I feel it. Happiness is like pain in this respect, rather than illness. 'If he feels happy he is happy (p. 15).

According to Wilson, if we deny that the wicked (the selfish, the drugged, etc.) are happy, it is because we feel that they ought not to be, rather than because it is conceptually impossible that they should be. A man may be narrow in his interests, inferior to others in various specifiable ways, precariously placed, amoral, immoral — no such considerations, however, make it logically impossible or inconceivable that he should be happy.

Wilson also touches upon the question of happiness as an end, tentatively arguing, as against Aristotle, that one can choose to be happy for some other end beyond happiness itself, and, conversely, that one can seek other ends for themselves without concern for happiness. (The latter proposition, also strongly argued by Kenny, would not, I think, have been disputed by Aristotle.) Yet, as he is forced to admit, the notion of somebody *choosing,* after much thought and deliberation, to have a happy life, is rather curious. Rather than conclude that it is not merely one end among many, however, he suggests that, though happiness does function as an adequate check to requests for reasons for action, nonetheless one might not deliberately pursue happiness in the sense of consciously set out to organise one's more immediate desires, pleasures and wants with a view to happiness. Happiness would thus appear to be an end so far as logic goes, but not necessarily a man's avowed aim in practice. To pursue happiness, he adds, is essentially to order one's desires rather than to seek indiscriminately to gratify all and any of one's various desires. That Platonic view is amplified by means of a distinction drawn between first level wants, which are those satisfied by the successful pursuit of pleasure (e.g. in smoking, I satisfy my want to smoke) and second level wants, which are those satisfied by the successful pursuit of happiness (e.g. in giving up smoking, I satisfy the want which came about as a result of my ordering my various competing and conflicting desires).

4.7 Wilson had asserted in passing that whereas 'specific emotions, like fear, normally have targets' or objects, in the sense that one is afraid of something, envious of somebody, etc., happiness does not. 'You can only be happy because of *X* or in the sphere of *X*: you cannot (so to speak) be happy at *X*' (p. 14). Lloyd Thomas offers a rather different view in his 1968 paper 'Happiness'.[16] Feeling happy, he agrees, is not necessarily related to any particular kind of object (as pride has to be related to something regarded as one's own); indeed it is not necessarily related to any object at all. Nonetheless it may have an object, as, for example, when one feels happy at the thought of a trip to Athens. Whether 'at' is here being used in the same way as was intended by Wilson is not perhaps entirely clear, but Lloyd Thomas does distinguish between an object of happiness and a reason for happiness. Thus 'I have just heard that my holidays will start next week' could be one's reason for feeling happy, while the object of one's feeling happy would be something like 'the thought of those lazy weeks in the sun' (p. 98).

The main purpose of Lloyd Thomas' paper, however, is to distinguish what he sees as four main uses of the term 'happy'. These are:

(1) use of the term to refer to a feeling, typically of fairly short duration;

(2) use of the term in expressions such as 'I am feeling happy about my job' where feelings are not (or not primarily) involved at all;

(3) a behaviouristic use, most common with the adverbial form, which implies something like 'with relish' or 'gleefully', as in 'The Leader of the Opposition happily delivered one devastating argument after another'; and

(4) use of the term to refer to a relatively long period, as in the comment 'he had a happy life'.

A somewhat similar classification had previously been adopted by Robert Dearden in his article 'Happiness and Education', where he distinguishes three senses (as he calls them, rather than uses), which correspond more or less to Lloyd Thomas' first, second and fourth uses.[17]

In elaborating his first use Lloyd Thomas takes a view akin to that of Wilson and Von Wright to the effect that

> we might regard *X*'s circumstances as depressing, dull, etc., but this will not count against *X*'s claim that he feels happy so long as *X* regards his circumstances favourably . . . however, if a person claims that he feels happy and then goes on to say that he sees virtually every aspect of his circumstances as being, dull, etc., then we have reason for doubting that he's happy. [p. 98]

He adds that feeling happy does not depend upon making any conscious judgement or assessment, nor on locating any reason for one's happiness. 'The necessary connection is between having the feeling and the projection of a certain set of attitudes to one's circumstances' (p. 99). (An act of judgement may enter the picture in as much as the act of making the assessment or judgement may itself alter one's feelings.) If a judgement happens to be the basis of a person's feeling happy, it must be a judgement to the effect that things are good. If on the other hand he just feels happy, with the result that he projects a favourable attitude to his surroundings, he need not believe that things really are good 'for he may be sufficiently self-conscious to see that they only seem good as a result of how he feels' (p. 100).

What is of particular interest is Lloyd Thomas' attempt to distinguish this, his first use, from his fourth. In the fourth use, we are told, a person is saying that his life has been good (not merely satisfactory) and one of the characteristics of this use is 'that it is applied by reference to a person's standards for the good life' (p. 104). But those standards are set by the character of the individual, so 'to say that I am happy is to say that the circumstances of my life measure up to my standards for a good life' (p. 105). First person judgements, therefore, are subjective in a sense, but can be mistaken. (I can think that my circumstances measure up to my standards and be incorrect in that assumption.) In the case of third person judgements, he concedes that the subject's sincere agreement that he is happy is a minimum condition of a correct judgement, but asks 'is it sufficient for agreeing that another man is happy that he says he is, or can we justifiably refuse to accept another's claim that he is happy?' (p. 106). He then reviews a number of different situations in which it might make sense to say 'he says that he is happy, but he's not really': the man might be telling a lie, ignorant of the meaning of the word, deceived about either his circumstances or his standards, or there might be a situation comparable to that in which 'a doctor deliberately deceives a patient as to the seriousness of an illness' such that 'even if the patient is successfully deceived we may be reluctant to allow that he is a happy man' (p. 106). This rather curious example leads Lloyd Thomas to say that in the fourth use an important feature is the subject's awareness of the actual circumstances in which he is placed now and is likely to be in the future. It is not, therefore, sufficient that the subject should *believe* that his life measures up to his standards for a good life. He must *know* it. There, it seems, lies the sting of this particular analysis. He draws the conclusion that treating happiness in the fourth use as an end is very nearly empty 'for it means no more than that the life can be judged in terms of the standards of the person who lived it' (p. 109). (He also suggests that when Mill says that by happiness he intends pleasure he might effectively be setting up pleasure as his standard for happiness in the fourth usage.)

Lloyd Thomas' paper is not an easy one to follow, but we cannot leave it without drawing attention to a suggestion that might form the basis of the argument I shall present below.

> It may be possible in the case of some feelings to give a complete account of the meaning of an expression of the form 'a feeling of *X*' in terms of the logical relationships between a feeling of *X* and various features of the circumstances, such as . . . the attitudes with which it is logically compatible or incompatible . . . [For example] feeling happy and feeling depressed are incompatible because an essential element in feeling happy is that things seem good, while an essential element in feeling depressed is that things do not seem good. [p. 100]

4.8 In a thorough and important article published in 1974, Theodore Benditt accepts that the word happy is sometimes used in ways that confirm Hare's account.[18] Nonetheless, he maintains, there are also other uses, 'in which a judgement that a third person is happy is a report about him which may be true or false' (p. 2) rather than an appraisal; similarly, first person statements may be true or false, although they involve appraisal.

Benditt proceeds from an examination of Von Wright's three ideals. He rejects each one of them in turn as being unsatisfactory. The Epicurean ideal cannot be the whole truth, because it just is not true that 'seeking pleasure in things is the only way to attain happiness'. The utilitarian ideal won't do because 'a person could conceivably have all of his needs and wants . . . satisfied and yet fail to be happy' (p. 3). His argument for that conclusion makes use of a distinction similar to that made by Montague between not being happy and being unhappy: achieving the utilitarian ideal might amount to avoiding unhappiness, but that is not the same thing as achieving happiness. The Aristotelian ideal is also dismissed: 'a person could conceivably have all of the necessities and spend his time doing what he did well and still find his life somehow hollow and even detest it. Such a person could not truly be said to be happy' (p. 4). Such ideals, then, may contain useful contingent prescriptions for achieving happiness, but they do not tell us what it is.

According to Benditt happiness is properly predicated of a person rather than a life. Failure to see this, he suggests, is what renders Lloyd Thomas' work on the concept unsatisfactory, for Lloyd Thomas assumes the ascription of happiness to someone to be largely a matter of appraisal, because he concentrates on the notion of a happy life, which must in some sense be a good life, which in turn demands that some appraisal should take place. 'He had a happy life' is ambiguous: it might mean either that he has been a happy man during his life, which presupposes nothing about a good life or standards, or that he has had a good or fortunate life, which obviously does. By talking of a happy man rather than a happy life, we avoid both the ambiguity and any assumption about standards being involved.

He makes the important observations that (a) any attempt to tie the concept of happiness to such things as ideals or the notion of the good life necessarily involves setting up criteria for happiness, and yet, (b) any criterion that anyone has yet suggested can always be meaningfully challenged. Thus, in reverse order, we can meaningfully challenge the view that having various possessions is a necessary condition of happiness, consequently it is unwise to attempt to encapsulate happiness in an ideal that is based on secure possession. He then tries to argue that Hare's attempt to have it both ways, seeing happiness reports as being both appraisals and reports on the subject's state of mind, involves an internal contradiction and raises the question of how, on this account, happiness can be recommended or used as a reason for action. For most of us the observation that by doing something we could make ourselves happy is likely, at the very least, to be an incentive. But by Hare's analysis a man might think himself happy, yet not be so in fact, because he is vicious and thereby fails to meet Hare's criteria for appraisal. Hare might want to set him straight and make him really happy. But on what grounds will he be able to shift the man? How can he persuade him, since he thinks he is happy, to change his ways and be truly happy? (This objection would seem to count equally against all views that seek to separate being and feeling happy.)

Benditt's own positive account is formulated as follows: 'a person *N* is happy (overall) throughout a period of time *t* if (and only if) *N* is satisfied with his life throughout *t*. *N* is satisfied with his life throughout *t* if (and only if) *N* is disposed, when he considers his life during *t*, to feel satisfied with his life' (p. 8). In elaborating this, Benditt first points out the ambiguity of 'being satisfied', which might mean either settling for something (as in 'are you satisfied with the arrangements?') or getting satisfaction from something (as in 'I get real satisfaction from the first drink after a game'). It is the latter, positive, sense that he has in mind, and he points out that this sense of satisfaction is conceptually bound up with one's hopes, expectations, demands, requirements, etc. 'It is the positive feeling of satisfaction and not just feeling free from dissatisfaction' (p. 9) that he is concerned with – the feeling following on a job well done, so to speak, rather than a mere absence of irritation. His final step is to distinguish feelings of contentment from satisfaction. 'Any number of things can make a person feel contented . . . One may just wake up feeling that way . . . A hot drink on a cold day can produce such a feeling, as can a good meal' (p. 10). That is to be distinguished from feeling satisfied with something, not in the sense of satisfied because of something (as one might be satisfied because of the fact that one has a steady job), but 'because one judges that the object of some expectation connected with one's job is realised' (p. 11). In other words, happiness, on this account, is conceptually tied to the feeling of satisfaction that arises out of seeing things the way you want them: 'A person feels satisfied with his life, if and only if he gets a feeling of satisfaction when he judges that his expectations in life are being attained' (p. 11).

From this account it follows, as Benditt explains, that to be happy it is logically necessary to make assessments; from that it follows that babies and young children cannot be happy, at any rate not in the same sense. He also thinks it inappropriate to regard the drugged or drunk man as happy, and suggests that we should distinguish a dispositional use of the word, implying that a person remains happy under normal conditions, and a more specific sense implying that someone is 'disposed under certain conditions' to feel happy. Returning to the theme of the ideal lives, he suggests that the Epicurean and the Aristotelian ideals represent extreme poles, either of which may be combined with the utilitarian ideal. He concludes by making a suggestion that introduces a new issue. The issue is that of the logic of comparative judgements in respect of happiness, and the suggestion is that the claim that *A* is happier than *B* has to be explained in one of three ways: *A* must be more overjoyed about something, or satisfied in more areas, or experience more intense feelings of satisfaction. He categorically denies any plausibility to attempts to explain comparative judgements in terms of differing ideals. 'Happiness is a matter of getting whatever it is that one wants and finding it worthwhile when one gets it' (p. 19).

4.9 In recent years two champions of a more Aristotelian view have appeared. In a paper published in 1975, Simpson challenges the view that a man is happy if he is able to get whatever he wants.[19] He draws a distinction between what one wants and what one really wants, which is not unlike the distinction that Wilson drew between first and second level wants. What one wants may be termed one's desires, and illustrations are provided by any typical daily want. What one really wants, what one wills, is that which one does in fact pursue, make sacrifices for, take active steps to procure, etc. Thus I want to smoke, yet I give it up or refrain. I certainly *do* want to smoke; that is one of my desires. But since I do not in fact do so, we must conclude that not smoking is the object of my will, my real want. Mere desires

> do not look beyond the particular object desired or the particular activity in which pleasure is taken: whereas, when as an object of a man's will a particular state of affairs or action is wanted or when satisfaction is found in some activity, it must always be in consequence of having some feature which is the sort of thing which the man in some general way, wants to exist, that is to say, a feature which makes the object or activity in some way seem good or worthwhile. [p. 172]

According to Simpson, happiness depends upon the satisfaction of objects of will, rather than mere desires, and he then goes on to argue that not only must objects of will be seen as worthwhile by the subject, but they must also really be worthwhile or valuable. His argument is that such things as friendship, health, sanity, wealth and freedom are necessary for normal human life. ('Any man has reason to want' them and to consider them 'part of human good' – p. 173.) But it is far from clear whether this is a logical or merely a necessary contingent truth and, consequently, whether the link between, say, friendship and happiness is the result of human nature being what it is or of happiness being what it is.

Finally, Goldstein makes a spirited attempt to uphold the view that there are certain material conditions that are necessary to happiness.[20] He complains that Wilson, in rejecting such factors as precariousness, inferiority and immorality as having no bearing on the concept of happiness 'offers no reason to support his denial' and no 'explanation of why people in fact do tend to use these criteria' (p. 531). People just do hesitate to say that Hitler was truly happy, because they just do think it odd to imagine villainy and happiness in the same person. 'Many people . . . [just do] deny that idiots or madmen could be happy . . . even if they do enjoy life. Some people have even said that disasters after one's death . . . would be reason to say the person does not have a happy life. Some refuse to call a man happy whose wife has been carrying on with another man' (p. 531). Given that, Goldstein suggests, rebuking Montague *en passant* for his remark that philosophers have been recommending different forms of happiness under the guise of saying what it is, it is more in keeping with both present and past usage and thought about happiness to include non-hedonic evaluative criteria in the concept, to regard ascriptions of happiness as essentially appraisals and to widen the repertoire of ways in which we may legitimately say of another that he is not really happy.

Now that we have gone almost full circle, and with the ghost of Aristotle back on the scene, it is time to examine the concept for ourselves.

PART II

Some Positive Conclusions

CHAPTER 5

The Concept Analysed

5.1 Many writers make reference to the etymology of the word 'happiness', often hoping to gain support for the idea that happiness is involved in some way with good fortune, just as the Latin word *felix,* sometimes translated 'happy', implies fortunate and the Greek word *eudaimon* has connotations of being favoured by the Gods. It is certainly true to say that the word happiness appears to derive from the archaic 'hap' meaning 'chance', 'luck' or 'good fortune'; and equally there have been in the past, and still are, uses of the term that strongly suggest this idea of good fortune. For example, expressions such as 'happily he arrived in time to avert the disaster', 'by a happy coincidence' or 'happy the man who dies peacefully in his bed' are not uncommon.

Nonetheless there seems no warrant for assuming that the concept of happiness that we are concerned with is necessarily logically tied up with the idea of good fortune. The fact that the word 'education' may derive from the Latin word *educare,* meaning to draw forth or lead out, cannot seriously be used as an argument to show that our conception of education must be based upon some notion of drawing out. So why should the derivation of the word happy be presumed to establish that what we now mean by 'happiness' must involve an element of good fortune? Etymology pertains to words; and words and concepts, though they march hand in hand, are clearly distinct. One word may sometimes be used in reference to several different concepts (e.g. the word bow: bow and arrow; bow on her hair). Conversely, one concept may be picked out by a number of different words, as pikelet and crumpet, drawing room and lounge or noir and black each do. We are concerned with the nature of happiness, which is to say with giving as detailed and explicit account as we can of what is going on if someone is happy or what it means to describe someone as happy; it may transpire that we do have reason to suggest that nobody could be happy without a degree of good fortune, but there are no grounds for assuming from the outset that the happy man must be blessed, least of all because the word we are using originally had such connotations. It may no longer have them or, more radically, we may sensibly argue that if the word still has such connotations in typical usage, it ought not to have, just as one might plausibly maintain that the connotations that the word 'anarchist' used to have (solitary individual, wide brimmed hat, long shabby coat, smoking bomb) are no longer appropriate, given the nature of those who are called and call themselves anarchists today. It is words, not concepts, that carry connotations. As usage of words changes, so too do connotations. Consequently past connotations of the word 'happy' do not necessarily tell us anything about the concept of happiness.

It is surely clear, as John Wilson states (4.6), that 'you *can* be happy without being . . . fortunate'[1] in the sense of having good luck, even though it may not happen very often. Some people may be happier in what most of us would regard as misfortune than others considerably better placed. It is possible, however difficult, to remain happy in apparent adversity.

5.2 While we are on the broad subject of the distinction between word and concept the question of whether it is legitimate or helpful to talk of different uses of the term happiness should be raised, and, if so, whether those different uses are necessarily different senses of the word. Lloyd Thomas,[2] it will be recalled, refers to four different *uses*, (4.7), the first exhibited in a phrase like 'I feel happy', referring to a passing feeling, the second in a phrase like 'I feel happy about the arrangements', the third in some such remark as 'he lashed about him happily' and the fourth in the remark 'he is a happy man'. Robert Dearden,[3] adopting a similar set of distinctions, but dispensing with Lloyd Thomas' third, refers to them as different *senses* of the word 'happy' (4.7).

It cannot be denied that different uses of the word, such as those listed, are possible, if by 'different uses' we mean no more than 'used in different contexts'. But it may prove misleading to think of these different uses as different senses of the word, since at this stage of the enquiry it must remain an open matter whether or not the word retains essentially the same sense in each context. Thus, even the adverbial usage, which at first blush looks quite distinct from the others, seems to have implications of satisfaction, pleasure and an 'everything going my way' feeling, which many would argue are what happiness is essentially about. Certainly it would seem to beg a number of questions to assume from the start that 'feeling happy' (implying a transitory agreeable mood) and 'being happy in life' involve different senses of happiness. It may turn out that we do want to make quite a sharp distinction between the nature of happiness in either case, but at the outset we have no warrant for making that assumption at all. It may just as well transpire that such difference as there is is fully accounted for by the phrases 'for a short period' and 'in a life-time'. In other words, being happy in life might have to be explained as no more than the repeated (or extended) experience of happiness over a short period. Or again, the crucial point might be that being happy in either context is equally a case of satisfaction or being pleased. It may be true, as Lloyd Thomas maintains, that his other usage ('I am feeling happy about the arrangements') refers to no feeling at all, but for all that has been said so far 'I am a happy man' and even 'I feel happy today' may not strictly speaking refer to a feeling either. Despite the undoubted fact that 'I am a happy man' and 'I feel happy about the arrangements' are to be distinguished, it could be that the difference is due to the difference between life and a set of arrangements rather than to different senses of 'happy'. Lloyd Thomas asserts (4.7) that when we say something like 'I feel happy' we make reference to 'something positive, to an overflow or surplus of agreeable states and things', which is not the case when we say 'I feel happy about the arrangements'.[4] But at this stage that is no more than assertion; and it may reasonably be countered: why do I have to refer to such an overflow or surplus whenever I claim to feel happy? Why could I not make such reference when I feel happy about something?

5.3 Any attempt at a preliminary classification of different senses of the word runs the risk of removing from our scrutiny contexts that may tell us something about the sense of the word (or senses if there *are* more than one) that we are interested in. It would be easier to begin by examining a concept and then, in the light of our examination, to draw conclusions about different uses and senses, than to prejudge the matter in this way. We should attempt to state what exactly we want to enquire into and proceed to examine that concept.

Presumably our interest, at least initially, is in the happiness that men may be said to seek, be enjoined to pursue or hope for throughout their lives, that which the poets, as we have seen, speak of; that which Alexander Pope explicitly and correctly points out (3.5) may be called a number of different names;[5] that which we tend to find diminished by great personal tragedy; that which tends to make people calm, smiling and at peace with the world; that which people tend to feel when they fall in love, do well or see their children prosper. We have to start with some such rough and hazy impressionistic picture as that, and from and into that launch our enquiry. If, at this stage, we take any notice at all of something like Aristotle's observation that one swallow does not make a summer, it must not be because we are only interested in the-whole-life-through sense of happiness, still less because we take it for granted from the start that true happiness is a life-long thing. It must be because we only happen to be interested in considering what is involved in living happily throughout one's life. (Incidentally, I use that particular phrasing because Benditt's suggestion (4.8) that happiness should be predicated of the man rather than the life is surely to be accepted.[6])

It is the concept of happiness, then, with which we are concerned – the notion of a man happy as he lives his life. What really is involved in that notion?

5.4 The first observation that needs to be made is that happiness is a *broad concept*, as, for example, are education and love. By a broad concept I do not mean a blurred concept, but a concept that is not of something simple and specific. The distinction is important. Some concepts are narrow, which is to say they are conceptions of something simple, specific and hence straightforward, as is the concept of a duck. By contrast the concept of animal is broad, because it is less specific. But that does not mean it is more blurred. Strictly speaking, no doubt, no concept is blurred – it is only our conceptions that are blurred. However that may be, something like Lewis Carroll's Snark, though a narrow concept, since it picks out a specific creature, is blurred compared to the broader concept of animal, since Carroll does not give us a clear image (deliberately, of course).[7] Education, love and happiness are all broad concepts because they do not pick out a single, simple activity, state of mind or state of affairs. Two people engaged in quite different tasks may nonetheless both be busy educating (or being educated). Two people may feel differently and yet both be in love. In just the same way, to say of two people that they are happy is not necessarily to insist that they are in an identical state of mind, despite the fact that it is to say the same thing about them. If proof of that very obvious contention were needed one has only to engage in a little introspection: on the various occasions that I have felt happy I have not necessarily been in exactly the same state of mind, if that means something like undergoing identical sensations. To say that happiness is a broad concept is to say that it cannot be identified with some single sensation or feeling.

5.5 To be distinguished from the above is a second preliminary observation and that is that the word happiness is a *degree word*. By a degree word I mean one that we apply in cases where it is applicable to a high degree, even though strictly speaking it is a term that picks out an absolute state. We talk about people being in love or out of love, kind or unkind and suchlike, as though it were a simple and absolute matter on a par with wearing shoes, which one either is or is not. In point of fact, of course, some of those people whom we claim to be in love are rather more so than others; amongst the kindly ones some are rather less so than others. We describe all people beyond a certain point as being in love or kind, notwithstanding difference of degree between them. In the same way, although presumably we may conceive of the completely happy man, and although we talk about somebody being happy as if it were an absolute state akin to being male or female, in practice we apply the term to those whom we take to be happy to a significant degree or in certain important respects.

Many people have drawn attention to the point that we tend to assess the happiness or otherwise of ourselves and others in respect of important aspects of their lives, but the point being made here is that that is a contingent feature of the way we use the word 'happiness', and not a logical feature of happiness. 'He is a happy man' is not synonymous with 'he is happy in respect of the important features of his life' and is not equivalent to 'he is satisfied in respect of the important features of his life'. Strictly speaking a happy man would be completely happy, i.e. satisfied in all respects. It is merely a matter of contingent fact, brought about by the sad state of the world, not by the logic of happiness, that we call people who are happy for the most part or happy in all essentials or happy in respect of important aspects of their lives, happy without qualification, just as we call people miserable who could be more miserable yet. This is to reject or at least to modify severely the contentions of Montague and Simpson (4.5, 4.9).[8] The former suggests that a large aggregate of pleasure over pain does not necessarily make you happy, since what matters is those pleasures you regard as significant in your way of life. The latter argues that the important thing is the satisfaction of what he terms objects of will – that is, what one really wants on reflection or something very close to Wilson's secondary desires – and that these objects of will must also be desirable in fact. The view that happiness is logically tied to the satisfaction of objectively desirable desires is, as I shall argue below, to be rejected out of hand. Montague's point is in a sense correct, but not far the reasons he presumes: it is not a matter of logic that what the individual sees as his significant desires must be satisfied for happiness – it is rather that being significant they count for more quantitatively. In other words, and allowing for the fact that happiness is a degree word, a man *is* happy insofar as he has a large aggregate of pleasure over pain, but he will not experience such an aggregate if what he regards as his crucial desires are frustrated.

5.6 I have suggested that happiness is a broad concept and that it cannot be identified with some single sensation or feeling. Wilson is therefore right to disassociate happiness from joy (4.6).[9] The two are not synonymous. Possibly it is the case that insofar as a man experiences joy he must at that time feel happy. But though the happy man may, therefore, feel joyful, he obviously does not have to. It is possible to feel happy without experiencing joy. Joy perhaps is a species of happiness, but it is not the whole of it or coextensive with it. In exactly the same way insofar as a man is ecstatic, satisfied, content, pleased, delighted and suchlike he may well be presumed to be happy, but being happy does not necessarily imply that he is specifically ecstatic or satisfied or delighted, etc. What, however, it surely does imply is that he experiences at least one of a group of such feelings. You cannot be happy and yet experience no feeling of satisfaction, delight, content, ecstasy, etc. Happiness, in other words, is a generic term, encompassing the many specific forms it may take or many species. It must, logically, involve some feeling or feelings, but it cannot be identified with any particular feeling or set of feelings.

The importance of this apparently obvious point is considerable. It indicates that research into happiness is not one and the same thing as empirical research into the nature of some one or other of such subjective feelings as those of ecstasy or joy. You do not necessarily need to establish that I am truly thrilled in order to establish that I am happy. It also means that important distinctions may be drawn between two people who are nonetheless equally happy: a man in ecstasy is quite different from a man who is quietly contented, but they may both be equally happy. A happy man does not necessarily spend his life on the exhilarating heights of joy nor yet on the calm plains of contentment. His life will very likely encompass both. To some extent this may be viewed as a matter for arbitrary decision as to what we wish to talk about–the wider state that encompasses specific feelings or some one or other of the specific feelings. But it would also seem to be a matter of fact that happiness is not generally conceived as being one with some specific type of feeling, and that much psychological research supposedly relating to happiness has in fact been directed to certain specific feelings or sensations, and has not therefore addressed itself diretly to the temperament or state of mind that most people have in mind when they think of people being happy.

5.7 At this point I would claim to have done no more than make explicit what we are trying to talk about — namely the state of mind that people may be in for shorter or longer periods, that, for all we yet know to the contrary, they may experience in relation to arrangements as well as anything else, but that, since theoretically we envisage it as a total state of mind, we will not in practice attribute to people unless we have reason to suppose them to experience it in respect of most important aspects of their lives, that might take the form of a sense of ecstasy or indeed any form or combination on a continuum from contentment to being thrilled, that we generally call happiness. The question is whether a fuller account of this happiness can now be given that will reveal something about its nature – something about the logical properties of the concept.

The first major issue to be considered is that of material conditions. Aristotle, as we have seen, gradually built up a list of external material conditions that were, he claimed, necessary for happiness. Friendship, virtuous behaviour and a certain amount of material wealth were all required. Whether Aristotle himself meant us to see some or all of these things as logically necessary (i.e. happiness would be literally inconceivable without them) or merely contingently necessary (i.e. happiness would not in fact ever be achieved without them) may not be clear (see above, ch. 2). But there is no doubt that some contemporary philosophers wish to argue that some material conditions are logically necessary. Thus Brian Barry denies that one who lives a vicious life could be happy, not merely as a matter of fact, but as a matter of the meaning of happiness.[10] Austin finds it inconceivable that the unkind should be happy (4.4). Hare asks us how we could possibly regard the mental defective as happy (4.4). Simpson and Goldstein emphasise the necessity of friendship and wealth (4.9).[11]

What is at issue here is whether such things as health, wealth, moral goodness and love are necessary to happiness in the same sort of way that not having a wife is necessary to bachelorhood, or whether, if necessary at all, they are necessary in the way that not having a wife may just happen to be necessary for members of a particular religious order. Granted many people may indeed need certain things like money, sex or good health in order to be happy, is that because of something about the nature of happiness or because of something about the way people happen to be? The difference between the two views is of enormous importance, because upon it may hinge the entire question of what policy to adopt if one wishes to increase happiness. If it is just a contingent matter of fact that people find their happiness under certain conditions, the situation might be altered so that they can come to find it or they might be altered in various ways. If the matter is one of logic, there is nothing that can be done, just as no amount of legislation or social engineering will enable a married man to be a bachelor at the same time. (One thinks here too of the question of what to make of theses like those of Bertrand Russell (3.8): are we to imagine him to be making a claim to the effect that family life does as a matter of fact make men happy or that it is conceptually tied to it?)[12]

It seems to me to be quite clear and certain that there are no specific material conditions that are logically necessary to happiness. That this is so is shown by the fact that it is perfectly intelligible, however unlikely, to imagine someone being happy in the absence of any proposed condition. A man might be poor, yet happy; he might be sick, yet happy; he might be friendless, yet happy; he might be unpleasant, yet happy; he might even have retired to bed to pass dried peas from one saucepan to another, yet be happy. We may think some or all of those instances exceedingly unlikely; we may be at a loss, ourselves, to understand how others could be happy under such or other circumstances, since *we* certainly could not be; we may find it hard to credit: but the fact remains that such things are conceivable, in a way that it is not conceivable that a bachelor should be married. If it is conceivable that people should be happy in such circumstances, then the proposed conditions of happiness are not logically necessary conditions.

Equally clearly there is no one condition or set of conditions that would be sufficient to establish that a person was happy. In other words there is no list of material conditions, *A, B, C* such that anybody who has *A, B, C* must *ipso facto* be happy. Here, as in the previous paragraph, it must be stressed that we are not talking about what may or may not as a matter of fact cause people to be happy. For all that has been said to the contrary so far, there may be a list of conditions *ABC* that would make anybody happy; but if that were so it would be a matter of contingent fact – something to do with the way human beings happen to be, which might conceivably change. Indeed, whether in fact there are some such conditions that are contingently necessary and/or sufficient to make men happy, men being what they are, is one of the things we shall ultimately want to know. But we will never get a clear answer to that question until we have a clear answer to this question: what is happiness? And in reply to that, at the moment, we are saying that there are no necessary material conditions and no sufficient material conditions: one could be rich, healthy, loved, etc., and yet be unhappy. We may object to calling the selfish man happy, find it hard to believe that the man without friends is happy, hope that the rich man isn't happy, assume that the famous man must be happy, refuse to accept that the revered and loved man isn't happy, and so on and so forth. What we cannot do is say that such examples are logically impossible ones.

But if that is the case, how are we to explain Hare's point (4.4) that we should nonetheless be inclined to say of the mental defective that he is not really happy, Simpson's specific list of goods (4.9) allegedly necessary for happiness and Goldstein's objection (4.9) that the view outlined here, like that put forward by Wilson, is put forward with no reasoning in support? Very simply: we do indeed, as Hare insists, tend to make judgements about other people's happiness as a result of making appraisals of their situation on our terms, but that does not mean that their happiness is to be decided by our appraisals or that we are correct to proceed in that fashion. No doubt we generally assess the calibre of politicians by reference to our appraisals of them conducted on our terms, but that does not mean that the actual calibre of a politician is to be decided by reference to our appraisal system. We don't like something about a particular politician perhaps and, in addition, we can't believe he can be happy. Whether he is a good politician and whether he is a happy man would seem to be two more entirely different questions.

Likewise, all that Goldstein has to say (4.9) to the effect that we do tend to say this and don't tend to say that may be true, but we are not and should not be governed by what people say, even though we do and should take some notice of it. We would not accept that pigs have wings just because people said they did, nor yet could we count the expression 'if pigs had wings' as conclusive evidence against their having wings. It is certainly the case, as Goldstein maintains, that many people feel uncomfortable about the idea of Hitler being happy; they don't want to admit the possibility that he might have been and they tend therefore to deny that he could have been. But the question of whether villainy is or is not compatible with happiness cannot be answered in this way, by reviewing what people tend to say, for that gives us only what people tend to think. The question can only be answered by diligently searching one's mind. Wilson offers no argument for his view that happiness 'is not conceptually tied to any set of facts about a man's situation in life' because there *is* no argument beyond the appeal for considered introspection. There is nothing more to do beyond observing that it appears quite intelligible, if unlikely or deplorable, that an evil man should nonetheless be happy. Of course Goldstein and others may continue to maintain that the case appears different to them. But this much can be said: whereas on his view there is no obvious explanation of why some people should maintain the opposite, on the view that I am putting forward a plausible account of why some should nonetheless take Goldstein's view is available – they don't want to admit that Hitler could have been happy for a variety of obvious reasons; or, to take another example, they recognise that the wife who doesn't realise that her husband is unfaithful is happy, if she is at all, as a result of delusion and that seems objectionable in various ways. In other words there are good reasons for *objecting* to people finding happiness in certain cases, but that is a different matter from there being good reasons for denying that somebody could be happy in those cases. There seems to be a confusion that consists in moving from the true belief that happiness is some kind of good to the conclusion that it cannot be associated with evil. But the fact is that repugnant causes may give rise to a good state of mind, and valuable things may be the product of evil.

To summarise the above. Judgements that people typically make about happiness are not conclusive evidence; what seems to be intelligible has to be treated as such. Some confusion probably arises from the ambiguity of a phrase like 'we should not say . . .', which might mean either 'as a matter of fact people like us don't say . . .', which proves little, or 'it wouldn't make sense to say . . .', which, if true, is strong evidence. Goldstein fails to see that Wilson's evidence is to be found by the intelligibility test and that his own comments are based on the other, unacceptable, linguistic test. Hare offers views that seem, on reflection, to fail by the intelligibility test, as does Simpson: it just is intelligible that a man should be happy and without friends, and so on. Whether as a matter of fact it is contingently possible or likely is another matter.

5.8 The same as has been said of material conditions is to be said of personal characteristics. There are no particular personality characteristics that are logically necessary to happiness, though again some may be contingently necessary. Thus selfishness may very likely militate against finding happiness in the world as we know it; conceivably it may make it quite impossible, in the world as we know it. But there is nothing logically odd, contradictory or unintelligible about the idea of a happy selfish man. Likewise such attributes as cleverness, patience, imagination, intellectual curiosity or dullness would seem to be neither necessary nor sufficient conditions of happiness. It is neither beyond belief, nor in fact outside experience, to find clever miserable people, dull happy people, dull miserable people and so on.

5.9 What is there that is logically true of happiness, if it has no material or personal necessary or sufficient conditions? There are two important logical features of the concept.

(1) First, happiness is something that only creatures with consciousness can experience. What is meant by consciousness in this context is the capacity to stand outside of oneself, seeing oneself as an actor in a situation, and to envisage that things might have been otherwise. Inanimate matter and programmed machines, however sophisticated, lack consciousness in this sense, and it is therefore meaningless to think of a happy computer or happy robot. On the other hand, indoctrinated people can, logically, be happy, for although, in extreme cases, the indoctrinated individual thinks in terms of a set of beliefs that have been implanted rigidly in his mind that does not stop him recognising that the world is such that things might have been otherwise. (The exception that proves the rule would be the case of the individual indoctrinated with a belief in absolute, crass, unyielding determinism. He, one might reasonably say, has no conception that things might have been otherwise and one might just as reasonably say that he is incapable of happiness or unhappiness: experience, for him, is just what it is. The notion of having some attitude towards the inevitable and immutable, some feeling of joy, exasperation, contentment or what have you, is as meaningless as the notion of being angry with a stone.) Consciousness is necessary to happiness, because happiness (or its opposite) comes into being with the emergence of desires, satisfaction and suchlike concepts that logically imply a degree of freedom and manoeuvreability in thought. The question of whether animals or young children can be happy is not really a question about happiness but the question of whether animals and young children have the requisite consciousness.

It is the consideration of consciousness that gives Hare's example of the mental defective such plausibility as it has. Although it seems unwarranted to insist that no mental defective could be happy, there surely must come a point at which the defect is so great as to render the idea of happiness (and unhappiness) for the individual in question scarcely intelligible. But what would make the difference would not be the degree of derangement so much as the degree of consciousness. A man might be as mad as a hatter and yet happy; but an apparently calm and sober individual might experience such diminished consciousness (i.e. be so incapable of registering the various features of the world he is in as alterables) that it would be unintelligible to regard him as happy. In much the same way, none of us while asleep or under the anaesthetic is in the domain of happiness/unhappiness, and it is reasonable to maintain that there comes a point prior to actually being asleep or anaesthetised at which the level of consciousness is so low as to make it likewise meaningless to ascribe happiness or lack of it to the individual. There is no suggestion here that the happy man must be conscious that he is happy, incidentally; it is only argued that he must be a conscious being. (On the question of being and feeling happy, see below.)

(2) The other logical feature of happiness is its incompatibility with a wide range of other concepts such as loneliness, agitation, depression, irritation, self-doubt, low self-esteem, guilt, remorse and regret. Although it would be difficult to produce a finite list of terms logically incompatible with happiness such as these, and although there are important differences between some of them, which makes it difficult to draw neat and tidy observations about happiness from examining them, it is apparent that all such terms have in common the fact that they are *both* relational *and* attitudinal terms: they both express a relationship between the individual and his circumstances and reveal an attitude to that relationship. Loneliness, for example, means *both* being alone *and* not liking it. Merely being alone is not necessarily incompatible with happiness, but being lonely is. Likewise depression tells you more than that a person is in adverse circumstances — it indicates that it's getting him down. To have low self-esteem is to be disappointed in one's abilities. To feel guilty is to take up an attitude in respect of what one has done or failed to do.

This feature of the logic of the concept suggests that the essence of happiness lies in having a favourable attitude towards whatever relationship one happens to have to one's circumstances. Von Wright was correct in his observation that 'to be happy is to be in a certain relationship . . . to one's circumstances of life, [but] happiness is not in the circumstances . . . but springs into being with the relationship'.[13]

5.10 In positive terms, then, happiness would seem to be or to involve seeing the world as one would like it to be. To be happy is to have a sense of enmeshment with one's world. Logically, the conditions that give rise to this sense of enmeshment might be of any sort. But it would be unintelligible to regard a man as happy insofar as he was unenmeshed with his world, as he would be, for example, if being alone made him lonely, if being unable to get away from the company of others frustrated him, if learning that his wife was having an affair upset him, and so on. He may of course be described as, or called, happy, notwithstanding the fact that he is a little lonely, somewhat jealous, etc., since happiness is a degree word. A man who is thoroughly contented in life, except for a slight sadness at the failure of his book of poems to meet critical acclaim ten years ago, will be regarded as happy, judged by the standards of this imperfect world. But strictly speaking he is not happy without qualification. Strictly speaking, insofar as the man who is 'a little lonely' is a little lonely, to that extent and in that respect he is not happy.

This may seem rather slight reward for our search. Perhaps it is: searching for the Loch Ness monster does not guarantee that there is one, and the success of the search is not to be identified with producing it. But in any case the importance of what is being said really lies in what is being denied here: to say that happiness is a sense of enmeshment is to deny that it can be identified with any particular feeling or any particular sources; it is to deny too that it is necessarily bound up with truth, morality or realism. It should by now be evident that a man might be misinformed about something or self-deceived and yet be happy. Indeed sometimes he may be happy precisely because he is deceived or deluded. The man whose happiness would be shattered were he to realise that his wife is having an affair with another man, is not perhaps to be envied, but he may be happy, and, if he is, it is his delusion that allows it. The attempt to deny this must surely be attributed to the fact that some people do not like to see happiness based on delusions and therefore try to stigmatise it as unreal. But, while it lasts, it is not unreal: it is merely precarious and based on ignorance.

It is difficult to escape the conclusion that it is the poets and in some sense the more erratic and emotional philosophers who have been nearer the mark about happiness than philosophers of the rigidly rational school. Plato seems to have had a more acute grasp than Aristotle; Rousseau was more or less spot on with his observation that 'a conscious being whose powers were equal to his desire would be perfectly happy . . . True happiness consists in decreasing the difference between our desires and our powers, in establishing a perfect equilibrium between the power and the will';[14] ignorance *can* be bliss, and Shakespeare is surely right to make Othello claim 'I had been happy . . . had I nothing known' (3.6).

This is also the place to comment on Butler's view (3.2) that happiness depends not on how high up a scale you are, but on the direction in which you are travelling. (Strictly speaking, as we have seen, it is not a question of a scale at all: you are either happy or not, but it is conceded that we use happiness as a degree word.) Butler is correct, and the reason he is correct is that what tempers one's attitude to one's circumstances is the direction in which one is travelling: having limited funds is more irksome if the future looks worse, less irksome if things are looking up. It depends on the direction in which you are tending, because on that depends your attitude to your circumstances.

5.11 Happiness is generally presumed to be an emotion, but it seems far from obvious that it should be so classified. Emotions are usually distinguished from feelings or sensations by reference to the fact that they involve some form of cognitive appraisal: a feeling of lust or sexual desire becomes an aspect of love when the object of the feeling is viewed in a particular way. A feeling that might be indistinguishable from a feeling experienced in anger or hate becomes part of the emotion jealousy when it arises in a particular context (or is thought to arise in a particular context, for my jealousy is nonetheless real because it happens to be misplaced). Being envious means having some feeling (who can say precisely what feeling?) as a result of thinking that someone else is doing better than oneself in some respect that matters to one. In short, one cannot have an emotion as such without interpreting a limited aspect of one's experience in a certain way. In addition, it is commonly held, emotions are associated with specific objects: one is angry with somebody or at something, afraid of somebody or something, etc.

Lloyd Thomas suggests (4.7) that happiness, though it is not necessarily related to any particular kind of object, can nonetheless have one, as when a person feels happy at the thought of a trip to Athens. As I remarked above, however, it is very unclear that the thought of a trip to Athens functions as an object in the same way that your stupidity may function as the object of my anger. Furthermore (as Lloyd Thomas is aware) happiness does not have to have an object in this way, whereas it would seem that other emotions do: if there is literally no object of your anger, envy, love or whatever, than strictly speaking you are not experiencing anger, envy, love or whatever. But one can just feel happy. Happiness does, it is true, involve interpretation in a way, since the happy man is one who sees his world being as he would like it to be. However, in the first place this interpretation is quite different in kind from that typically associated with emotions: normally emotions are constituted by specific interpretations of limited situations, whereas here we are dealing with an overall estimate as to the acceptibility of one's life. Secondly you cannot, typically, experience an emotion without conscious articulation of the interpretation in question: you can't be jealous if you are not conscious of a certain state of affairs being such as you interpret them to be. By contrast you can be happy without being conscious that your affairs are as you would like them to be — 'conscious' here meaning consciously articulated rather than merely sensed. Othello would, and should, be surprised, if he is asked whether he sees the situation as he does; of course he does, that is what it is to be jealous. But the happy man may quite reasonably be asked whether all is as he would like it to be, for although it must be so (although he must sense it as such), he need not have articulated as much to himself, as a necessary condition of feeling happy. It follows from these observations that happiness is not entirely like other emotions and therefore either should not be classified as one or, alternatively, should be recognised as an emotion unique among emotions.

5.12 Are ascriptions of happiness, then, appraisals or statements of fact? Are they essentially judgements as to whether one's chosen evaluative criteria are being met, or descriptive assessments of whether objective criteria are being met? In practice there is no doubt that we very often treat happiness ascriptions as appraisals. So there is at least this much truth behind the appraisal view: people do deny or ascribe happiness to others in the light of their own view of the terms on which it is acceptable to be happy. People do proceed as if one could only be happy on their chosen terms. But in strict logic the case is different.

A true account of the matter is this. First person utterances are reports on one's own state of mind or feelings, which can be true or false. I can say that I am happy and be telling a lie, for instance. They involve judgement in the minimal sense that one has to categorise one's feelings (as being happy rather than wretched, so to speak), but they do not involve appraisal in the sense of assessment of the conditions in which one finds oneself. In order to state that I am happy, I do not need to examine my circumstances and check that they meet certain criteria. In logic, whether one is happy is a matter to be settled by introspection on one's state of mind.

Third person judgements likewise are strictly speaking statements that are either true or false. Whether he is happy is in no way a matter to be decided by reference to evaluative criteria of mine or in terms of appraising in the sense of evaluating his position. The statement that he is happy is either true or false (ignoring the question of degree) regardless of who makes it, and its truth or falsity depends once again on his state of mind.

It follows that there is no way of establishing for certain whether someone is happy apart from asking him, assuming even then that he is willing and able to speak the truth (for there are a limited number of ways in which the agent may make a mistaken claim about his happiness; see below 5.16). For practical purposes we may choose to take various behavioural signs such as lack of interest or weeping as indicators of unhappiness (the most general sign would be the tendency to reject or withdraw from a situation); or we might, if we chose, measure pleasure responses in the brain. But neither procedure could be relied upon to reveal the truth, both being logically subordinate to the agent's honest statement of how he feels. A man is not necessarily unhappy because he weeps or seems uninterested, and even an observed pattern of rejection might have some other explanation besides unhappiness. Physical sensations of pleasure, which are what we might measure in the brain, are not identical with a sense of enmeshment and could theoretically coexist with an overall state of unhappiness (see below 5.15; 6.9).

5.13 As we have seen, people might be indoctrinated and happy; they might conceivably be indoctrinated into happiness. That would be possible because indoctrination involves controlling thinking rather than bypassing it or obliterating it. One could therefore, in principle, enhance people's happiness by making them believe that all is for the best in the best of all possible worlds. (There's not much doubt that Candide was happy, even if some think he paid a rather high price for it.) What one could not do is programme people to happiness by a process of conditioning them into acceptance of their lot and unreflective resignation. Insofar as a person is conditioned into unthinking acceptance (as opposed to indoctrinated into a system of acceptance thoughts) he is not happy. By conditioning responses we bypass thought and that cuts out the vital condition of consciousness. The often debated issue of whether the masses in Aldous Huxley's *Brave New World* or George Orwell's *1984* are truly happy can now therefore be given a tentative answer: insofar as either author wishes us to imagine the majority as conditioned automata, their lack of complaint is not to be construed as an indication of happiness. Insofar as either one imagines that the majority has been indoctrinated into acceptance of the regimes in question, it is clear that we must assume it to be happy, whatever Huxley or Orwell may have intended.

To say that indoctrination could be a successful means to happiness is neither to recommend that way nor to say that it is the only way. It is certainly not the only way, and indeed in an open and free society, such as ours attempts to be, there is a case for saying that the antithesis of indoctrination, namely an attempt to provide knowledge, truth and understanding, would be of crucial importance. As I shall argue in the final chapter, given the nature of happiness, *in an open and changing society*, such attributes as realistic perceptions and expectations will be a great asset; for happy people are those who can come to terms with the society in which they find themselves, which suggests that flexibility and a grasp of the realities of a changing situation will be crucial in rapidly changing circumstances. (It has been conceded that happiness can coexist with or even be based upon delusion, but that is not to say that it is a secure or wise way in which to gain happiness.)

5.14 The question of the senses in which there may be degrees of happiness is to be distinguished from the point that happiness is a degree word. Here we are concerned with the ways in which it may be meaningful to make comparative judgements of the type 'I am happier than I was' or 'She is happier than him'. First, one may be more or less happy in the sense of more or less *widely* enmeshed. Secondly, one's sense of enmeshment may be accompanied by or take the form of more or less *intense* feelings drawn from the continuum between ecstasy and quiet content. Benditt's additional suggestion that one might be more or less contented in some sense other than more or less widely or more or less intensely happy I find difficult to comprehend. But his conclusion is absolutely correct: 'there is no ideal of life which is such that a person who lives it successfully is necessarily happier . . . than a person who successfully lives another sort of life'.[15] We must note as well that, though we may talk of *X* being happier than *Y* in the sense that *X* experiences a more intense feeling, logically the ecstatic or overjoyed person is not necessarily any happier than the contented person. He is indeed more overjoyed, his happiness takes a more extreme form, but he is not thereby any happier. No more is the new-found passion of young lovers any more love than the calmer feelings of an older couple, for all that it obviously is a great deal more intense.

What I have argued for is a conception of happiness in line with what Von Wright categorises as the utilitarian ideal, which, incidentally, as Benditt appreciates, is quite compatible with the other ideals Von Wright refers to as distinct. 'Happiness on such a view is essentially contentedness – an equilibrium between needs and wants on the one hand and satisfaction on the other.'[16] Inevitably the question must be faced of whether it is not indeed contentment that I have described and not happiness – not 'real' happiness as Goldstein would say. Is there not a distinction between happiness and contentment, and have I not confused them?

I am inclined to counter that question with one of my own: what kind of an objection is this supposed to be? It suggests that there are two things, distinct and plain for all to see, and that I have wrongly attributed the name of one to the other, as a man might describe a game of chess and wrongly refer to it as draughts. But surely the matter is not like that at all.

It seems to me that the objection that I have described contentment rather than happiness is a mere playing with words, and that what is needed here is no more than a conscious decision about whether to use words in one way or another (which way being in itself neither here nor there). We want to make people happy and minimise their unhappiness, let us suppose. Now one might specifically add that one actually wanted to increase the intensity of their feeling, to make them experience joy or ecstasy rather than render them more well-pleased or more contented, but I see no warrant for asserting that the former *is* happiness in a way that the latter is not. It is true that our language involves distinct usages for the terms 'happiness' and 'contentment'. Thus, as Montague correctly observes (4.5), it is usual to talk of being 'wildly happy' but not of being 'wildly contented'. This shows that the words 'happiness' and 'contentment' are not exactly synonymous. It does not show that happiness cannot be adequately characterised in terms of contentment, provided that one allows that one could be happy and more than contented. Certainly, using this same test of language (despite my misgivings about it), one can be 'contentedly happy' or 'happy in the sense of contented'. The truth is surely that one may be 'wildly happy', meaning something like 'happy and delirious with joy', or 'contentedly happy', but in either case *one is happy.* The fact is that a phrase like 'positively pleased', which Montague rightly insists is an aspect of happiness, is very unclear. The happy man does have to be positively pleased about life, if that means that he must have this sense of enmeshment (and not, for instance, just be insensate), but he does not have to be positively pleased, if that means that he has to be ecstatic or in seventh heaven. Given these considerations, it seems to me sensible to regard contentment as a species of happiness and to request those who want to confine themselves to talking of ecstasy and intensely thrilling sensations to say as much, rather than attempt to appropriate the word happiness for their own purposes.

A related issue is that of the exact relationship between happiness and unhappiness and the question of whether they are contraries or contradictories, whether, that is to say, removing unhappiness is the same thing as providing happiness. Sometimes this question is linked with the previous one, it being argued that a person could be not unhappy and yet not happy either, since he lacks any intense positive feelings. But in point of fact the questions can be separated, since one could equally well argue that a person might be not uncontented and yet not content. The problem in essence has nothing to do with language or what terminology we choose to employ; it is rather a matter of whether we can make sense of the idea of a neutral state of mind that is neither pleased nor displeased, neither content nor discontented, or neither happy nor unhappy. As so often, there is no doubt that we talk as if it were intelligible, but this may merely show yet again the limitations of ordinary language philosophy (3.2). The currency of the phrase 'a neutral state of mind' does not guarantee that it is possible for one's state of mind to be neither happy nor unhappy, or that the phrase has intelligibility at all.

It is certain that there may be states of mind that are so far from either extreme that we do not know for certain how to classify them. If that is what neutral means, then there are neutral states of mind. But if that is what neutral means, then it will not follow that happiness and unhappiness are contraries rather than contradictories so that removing people's unhappiness does not make them happy. It will only follow that there is a point at which we are not sure whether we really have removed their unhappiness and rendered them happy.

The true picture I imagine to be something like this: a scale leading from ecstasy or intense happiness at one end to misery or intense unhappiness at the other. The top half of the line would represent varying species of happiness, increasing, towards the top, in intensity, but not of course in happiness; the lower half would represent varying species of unhappiness, likewise increasing in intensity, perhaps becoming more unbearable but not becoming any the more instances of unhappiness. In the middle of the line there is no neutral state – just a point at which satisfaction accompanied by the mildest of feelings becomes dissatisfaction accompanied by the mildest of feelings. The fact that we cannot actually measure or detect the transition point does not seem to me to constitute any objection to looking at the matter in this way.

In other words, whereas, by contrast, love and hate are contraries, so that one may cease to hate someone without coming to love them, happiness and unhappiness are contradictories, so that a movement away from one is automatically a movement towards the other. (It should be added that consciousness in the sense previously outlined is taken for granted in the above remarks: it *is* possible to make someone not happy, without making them unhappy, or vice versa, by depriving them of consciousness.) Before leaving this matter, attention should be drawn to the attempt of Bradburn and Caplovitz to distinguish between people's positive and negative feelings. They claim to have found no relation between positive and negative items on their research questionnaire, which would lend some support for the thesis that happiness and unhappiness are merely contraries. However, W. Wilson has adequately shown that they failed to construct items that were true polar opposites (which would be crucial to make the point that happiness and unhappiness are contraries rather than contradictories) and claims that his own research indicates that polar opposites do correlate negatively.[17]

5.15 One other basic and fundamental point to be clarified at this point is the relationship between pleasure and happiness. A common mistake is that of failing to observe an ambiguity in the word 'pleasure': we may use it either to refer to a pleasurable sensation such as sexual release or scratching away a tickle, or to refer to pleasurable states of consciousness brought about by doing something or undergoing some experience. The range of activities that might conceivably bring about pleasure in the second sense is coextensive with human activity: it might be brought about by writing books, staring at a sunset, playing football, singing opera or indeed by participation in activities that also involve pleasure in the other sense.

Clearly happiness is not synonymous with pleasure in either sense: you can experience sexual pleasure frequently without necessarily being happy, and you can thoroughly enjoy (i.e. take pleasure in) the opera, staring at sunsets or anything else and not necessarily be happy. The major point of difference is that we use the word pleasure more specifically and to refer to something more immediate and concentrated than we do the word happiness. This is not to reintroduce the misleading distinction between a passing feeling of happiness and being happy over a period of time. It is a humdrum but accurate observation about how we generally use words: it is linguistically unusual, and to that extent inappropriate, to describe something so brief and localised as an orgasm as a feeling of happiness, or to describe one's response to something so specific as a night at the opera as a feeling of happiness. But if happiness and pleasure are not synonymous, largely because of the way they differ in specificity, what is the relationship between them? Some have tried to argue that pleasure is merely one possible source, but no guarantee of happiness; in support of that view it is suggested that a man experiencing many pleasures might nonetheless remain unhappy, while conversely a man might be happy yet experience relatively few pleasures. This latter suggestion, which takes us back to the consideration of whether an aggregate of pleasure is enough to ensure happiness (see above 5.5), is in itself quite correct, but it does not establish the main point. The truth is that happiness consists in pleasures in the second sense (which may or may not be closely allied to pleasures in the first sense) or, to rephrase it without changing the precise nature of the claim, such pleasures constitute or are ingredients, necessary and sufficient, in happiness. But it does not follow from this, as we saw above, that the more pleasures you experience the happier you are. Rather what matters is neither quality nor arithmetic quantity, but comprehensiveness judged in terms of the individual's perspective. You are the more happy insofar as the more pleasures that you regard as important are satisfied. The basic point can be well made in terms of John Wilson's distinction (4.6) between first and second order wants. A life that involved the satisfaction of very many simple desires (e.g. desire for sex, cigarettes, going to operas) gives us many pleasures (in both senses). But to be happy you need to experience pleasurable states of mind in respect of what is really important or what takes relative priority in your judgement. Thus it might be that, you being who you are, reflection and organisation would lead you to recognise that on balance you don't want to smoke (despite having an unambiguous desire for cigarettes), on balance satisfying your sexual craving brings you more anxiety and guilt feelings than it's worth, and going to operas just isn't giving you what a lazy life devoted to drinking and reading thrillers would. That is to say your second order wants (your 'objects of will' as Simpson termed them or something close to 'real needs' in Aristotle's terminology) are different, and they need to be satisfied to gain happiness.

In a sentence: happiness consists in pleasurable states of mind as a matter of definition, but men being what they are and 'happiness' being a degree word, what we mean by happy people are people whose second order wants are preponderantly satisfied.

5.16 Are we to say that 'if a man really thinks that he is happy . . . then it must surely be conceded that he is happy'?[18] And, conversely, are we to say that he cannot be happy unless he recognises that he is? Or are there ways in which a man can be mistaken about his own happiness? To put the matter in the form of a more general question, raised by Goldstein: in what circumstances, if any, would it be legitimate to insist that somebody was not really happy, whatever he said to the contrary (or, conversely, was really happy, whatever he said to the contrary)?[19]

There are one or two simple and immediate answers that may be given. The statement 'I am happy' may clearly be false, if the speaker is deliberately telling a lie or pretending. Again it may be false in the unlikely circumstance of the speaker being ignorant of the meaning of the word 'happy'. It must also be allowed that mistakes of a kind may arise as a result of faulty comparisons. Given that 'happy' is a degree word (i.e. used absolutely where strictly speaking there is only a high degree of happiness) I may claim to be happy when such a claim is *inconsistent* with my normal standards for judging myself happy, or I may claim to be happy now, but subsequently come to appreciate that what I then experienced was so much less in degree than I am capable of that it should not have counted as happiness. (Presumably one *might* also confuse what most people would regard as a well-nigh insensate state with a sense of enmeshment, but, apart from its inherent unlikeliness, the sheer impossibility of recognising a case of this kind of mistake would seem to make it hardly worth considering.)

The above are surely the only ways in which a first person judgement about happiness may be mistaken, and the following further candidates are to be otherwise explained.

(1) The situation in which a person claims to be happy, but we know that he holds some false belief about his situation, such as that his wife is faithful to him when in fact she is not. Of course we may very reasonably observe that 'he wouldn't be happy, if he knew the truth', 'he won't be happy for long' or 'his happiness is based on a delusion'. But no such observation alters the fact that he is happy despite the fact that or even, as the poet suggests, *because* he is in ignorance. A building is no less a building because it is built on insecure foundations, although it may not remain one for very long. A particularly important point to note here is that to insist that this man is not really happy would commit one either to writing into the concept certain necessary material conditions (i.e. absence of faithless wife as a necessary condition of happiness) or to making

certain claims about human nature (i.e. people with faithless wives cannot be happy). If some such assumption is not made, there are no grounds on which to raise the suggestion that the deluded man cannot really be happy. Yet the first alternative is absurd, and both alternatives can be empirically invalidated.

(2) A slight complication may be thought to arise in cases where the agent is not so much ignorant as self-deluding – where he does, in some sense, know that his wife is unfaithful, but won't face up to it. The cloudiness and obscurity of the concept of self-deception make this a difficult suggestion to deal with, but surely we must still say that, if, and insofar as, he successfully deceives himself, whatever that may involve precisely, he remains happy. Disagreement, one suspects, arises over an example like this because of the confusion between the idea that happiness is a good and the idea that it is good for people to be happy. Happiness on these terms, it may be felt, is undesirable. But, even if that is true, it does not follow that it is a bad state of mind and hence not happiness. The state of mind remains desirable; it is the terms on which it is obtained, the factors that give rise to it in this instance, that are bad. One may as reasonably distinguish between happiness and the circumstances that give rise to it, as one may between a book and the circumstances that give rise to it. Nietzsche's view that 'untruth is the condition of happiness' may be cynical and overstated; but it correctly recognises that happiness can be based on falsehood.

(3) Goldstein suggests that an individual might have a 'false belief as to the degree of satisfaction'[20] he is receiving. The difficulty here lies in interpreting the phrase 'degree of satisfaction'. If it is used to cover either extent or intensity of feeling it is difficult to see how the agent could be mistaken, except in one of the ways referred to above. (Incidentally the degree of intensity of feeling will not affect the amount of happiness anyway.) Presumably the agent could make a mistaken prediction about the duration of his feeling of satisfaction, but that does not make his present claim to happiness false. I do not see any other way to interpret the claim.

(4) Lloyd Thomas suggests that one might deceive oneself about one's standards for the good life and thus be led to make mistaken judgements about one's happiness.[21] Thus I might think that the single state is necessary to my happiness and refuse to recognise that marriage is part of my ideal. Such a case would seem to be an instance of self-deception, and the fact remains that insofar as I

succeed in deceiving myself I shall remain happy single, because happiness depends upon a correlation between what you get and how you perceive it, rather than on what is the case. Admittedly, if such a person were subsequently to marry, he might find that he was equally or more happy (in the ways allowable), but that does not mean that he could not also be happy now. (Slightly different would be the case of the person who isn't happy now and thinks that he would be if married, but who subsequently turns out to be mistaken in that thought. That example is obviously a case of faulty prediction rather than false judgement.)

(5) One thing that one may indeed be mistaken about is the cause of one's happiness, but such a mistake will not lead one to feel any the less happy. No doubt many of us, even when happy, do not understand why we are, give false accounts of why we are, or even candidly confess that we don't know why we are. But that is immaterial to the point in hand. Being happy does, perhaps, logically necessitate being able to recognise oneself as such when one reflects on the matter. But it certainly does not necessitate being able to account for one's happiness fully and accurately.

(6) It cannot be denied that the statement 'he is not really happy' is sometimes used to mean 'he is not what I would call happy'. The crucial point here is that, given all that has been said, in particular that there is no good reason to write any particular evaluative criteria into the concept of happiness, the phenomenon of people speaking in that way cannot be taken to show that the original subject may be mistaken. The fact that some of us will not use the word happy except on certain conditions does not show that people cannot in fact be happy except on those conditions. The fact that some of us may believe, sincerely and correctly, that we couldn't, shouldn't or wouldn't be happy except on certain conditions (which would explain why we might deny that anyone else could be) does not show that others could not be. The fact that we sincerely find it hard or impossible to conceive of anyone being happy except on certain conditions constitutes nothing in the way of support for that view. To claim otherwise would be to succumb to the temptation to impose an arbitrarily objective conception of happiness on the world: objective, because it would have public criteria set up for it; arbitrarily, because they would merely be those criteria selected by the individual in question (e.g. 'I wouldn't call any single man happy' arbitrarily imposes the criterion of marriage

as an objective condition of happiness).

(7) Finally, we should take note of the interesting example introduced by Lloyd Thomas. He asks us to imagine

> the situation in which a doctor deliberately deceives a patient as to the seriousness of his illness. Even if the patient is successfully deceived we may be reluctant to allow that he is a happy man. We are pulled two ways by such cases . . . The doctor might justify what he has done by saying that he wanted his patient to have a happy last six months of his life. On the other hand we might well feel that we would hate to be in one of those situations, and there is something seemingly paradoxical about saying that a person is happy but we would hate to be in his position.[22]

This line of thought leads Lloyd Thomas to say that to be happy in a real sense one needs to be aware of and to know both one's present and future circumstances as they really are (will be), rather than as one conceives them to be. But the reasoning here seems both absurd and unnecessary. We might indeed (though we might not) hate to be in the situation of the patient (i.e. dying, but unaware of it). But there is nothing paradoxical at all about recognising that someone else is happy in circumstances that we would not want to be in. We might not *want* happiness based on delusion for ourselves, but that does not mean either that others or that we cannot *be* happy as a result of delusion. The question of how the doctor may try to justify his procedure has nothing to do with the matter, just as the fact that this particular example involves some *prima facie* unpleasant circumstances does not. There may or may not be awkward situations to be faced in life; there may or may not be justification for dealing with them in one way or another; and one way of dealing with them may or may not appeal to us. But each of those issues is distinct and none of them has any bearing on whether or not we can fault an individual who in those circumstances claims that he is happy.

5.17 My argument, then, is that there are only a few ways, which can be specified and which are not of great significance, in which a person can be mistaken about whether he is at the present time happy. More than that, I would now suggest that, even though in rare cases the individual can be mistaken, being and feeling happy are logically inseparable, so that if you feel happy you are happy, and if you are happy you feel happy. In other words the kind of mistake that can occur in happiness judgements will apply equally both to feeling and being happy. (If you don't know the meaning of the word, for example, you may be mistaken, but you will make the same mistake about both being and feeling happy.) This is to oppose the view of people such as Austin and McPeck that one might be happy but not feel happy.[23] McPeck suggests that

> it is significant that Barrow does not treat expressions such as 'I think that I am happy' or 'I believe that I am happy' in his discussion of happiness. Presumably on his analysis [because it involves treating being and feeling happy as inseparable] such expressions would be nonsense in much the same way as 'I think I am in pain' might be nonsense. The fact remains, however, when anyone asks me if I am happy, I often say I don't know.[24]

McPeck thinks that happiness and pain are not analogous and that happiness 'is more akin to other emotions such as love or jealousy or anxiety',[25] and emotions, he claims, are fundamentally corrigible – we can make mistakes about our experience or alleged experience of them. Having a certain emotion does not entail that the person in question will feel it; in the same way, being happy does not entail feeling happy, although McPeck is prepared to concede that feeling happy does entail being happy.

However, there is, I think, confusion here, which arises out of the ambiguity of the phrase 'feeling happy'. 'I feel happy' might mean *either* I think or believe that I am happy *or* I am having a particular experience or I sense something that is the experience normally associated with the word happiness. 'Do you feel happy?', in other words, might be taken as an enquiry into whether you are in a certain state of mind or into whether you are aware of it being such. That one can be happy and not aware of it as such, inasmuch as one does not believe that one is happy, has been implicitly admitted above. In fact, in this sense of 'feel happy', I have argued that one could feel it without being it. Because it is possible in a limited number of ways to be mistaken about one's happiness or lack of it, it is possible to be happy and not know that one is or to believe that one is and not be so. Certainly, therefore, 'I think that I am happy' or 'I don't know whether I am happy' are not nonsense. They are legitimate turns of phrase that have their appropriate uses, essentially when slight or extreme caution is called for on the part of the speaker as a result of one or other of the circumstances enumerated above.

What, however, one cannot logically accept is that a man might be happy without having the sense of enmeshment (the feeling whatever form it may take), that is happiness, and conversely one cannot have that sense and not be happy. So in this sense feeling and being cannot be divorced. And the point of this observation is that it indicates the fact that the manner whereby a person achieves happiness is neither here nor there, so far as the question of whether he is happy goes. If the drug-addict, by means of drugs, gets himself into a state such that he has a sense of enmeshment, he is happy. If he is truly happy, he must have such a sense. Once again, to deny this, to successfully divorce being and feeling happy, not only contradicts the idea that the happy man should be characterised in terms of this sense of enmeshment; it also logically implies that some necessary conditions can be written in. For the only reason one could have for wanting to deny the conclusion is the feeling that somebody ought not to count as happy on certain terms, whatever he feels and whatever state of mind he is in.

McPeck's view that happiness is a straightforward emotion like any other has already been denied (5.11). As we have seen it does not have an object in the way that emotions typically do, and classification of one's state of mind as happy is not dependent on a specific form of appraisal, as is the case with typical instances of emotions. But we may in any case raise the question of whether what McPeck has to say about an emotion like jealousy is quite right. He suggests that jealousy is corrigible: I may make a mistake about it. For example, he observes, I may have no good grounds for my jealousy, whatever I feel. That is certainly correct, and one would willingly accept talk of misplaced or unfounded jealousy. But surely that *is* the sort of talk we should (and would) engage in: he still feels jealous and he still is jealous. It is just that he has no good reason to be so. But could not McPeck still hold to the restricted thesis that I can be jealous, without feeling it? Only, I suggest, in the sense that I can be jealous without realising that that is the appropriate term to describe the state I'm in. In other words I can be jealous without feeling jealous in the sense of being conscious that what I am experiencing is what is known as jealousy. But could I not actually be jealous, according to my psychoanalyst, who realises that it is because of my jealousy that I criticise my wife and her lover, without feeling it? Without feeling *what*? It is unintelligible to me to suggest that, though I have no sense of anything other than, let us say, love for my wife and affection for my friend, I am in fact jealous of them. At the very least I should require a convincing argument to the effect that subconsciously I don't love or like them – but that is tantamount to saying that it is subconsciously that I feel jealous. That in turn gets us into a quite different argument about the plausibility of the idea of subconscious states of mind and does not touch the present issue. My point here is simply that being jealous, consciously or subconsciously, is meaningless if no feelings of jealousy come into play (granted that emotions cannot be exclusively characterised in terms of feelings).

5.18 The importance of the question of whether being and feeling happy can be divorced lies in its relation to the question of whether the individual is necessarily the best judge of his own happiness, and hence with such questions as who should determine what it is best to do in the interests of happiness. To take one extreme, if the individual cannot be mistaken about his own happiness, we should obviously ideally consult with every individual; to take the other extreme, if the individual is as likely to be mistaken as not, we may reasonably take less account of him. Now, as we have seen, it is quite clear that the individual agent is not infallible when it comes to the question of his own happiness, and McPeck is quite right to stress as much. Nonetheless there are only a few strictly limited ways in which he can be mistaken, and given that if he feels happy he must be, whereas if he does not he cannot be, he is in practice the obvious authority to turn to on the matter. Provided the agent knows what 'happiness' means (that it denotes what I term a sense of enmeshment) and is not faced by problems of comparison, it is difficult to conceive of anyone better placed to determine whether he is or is not happy.

That, at any rate, would be my view so far as judgements about one's present happiness go. Predicting one's own future happiness is of course another matter, as Von Wright points out.[26] Prediction about one's own future happiness depends upon knowledge of a lot of things besides what happiness is and the state of mind one is in. It depends upon knowledge of oneself, knowledge of the likely possibilities and likely consequences of alternative courses of action, and the imaginative ability to project oneself into the future in a realistic way. As a matter of contingent fact, then, some people may be worse judges of what would make them happy than some third party who is well-informed and knows them well might be. But even in these cases the agent would have to be accepted as the final arbiter of the accuracy of any given prediction. Note also that the kinds of limitation the individual might have when it comes to predicting his own future are the sort that could in principle be remedied; the third party, on the other hand, will never be in a position to pronounce authoritatively on whether a prediction was in fact accurate.

All in all, then, the agent is in a relatively strong position when it comes to happiness judgements. He alone can determine whether he was or is happy; there is no logical reason why he should not also be the best person to predict his future happiness and he is certainly the final arbiter of any such prediction. But his honoured position does not imply that others could not as a matter of fact make accurate judgements about his happiness or lack of it (past, present and future). For when it comes to the business of making specific third person judgements about happiness there are a number of clues and pointers that it is reasonable to follow: in practice one may draw conclusions from such behaviour patterns as crying, anguished shrieks, a glum face, etc., although obviously such signs are not foolproof: the person in question may be acting, deceiving, crying for joy, or not in fact crying at all and so on. Again, up to a point, for practical purposes one may base one's judgements on what one knows of human nature and familiarity with particular circumstances: if my elder brother's wife has walked out on him, it is a safe bet that that will make him unhappy, whereas I would not be so sure in the case of my younger brother. We can also base our judgements on what the people in question say: other things being equal, if they claim to be depressed, envious, anxious or such like we may infer that they are not happy. The main feature of the above strategies is that they are reliable pointers in normal circumstances but not guarantees. There is however one type of behaviour that surely is an infallible pointer to unhappiness, and that is rejection. Given what happiness is, it follows that insofar as one rejects some aspect of one's situation one is to that extent less than happy. To reject or seek to escape is logically to deny that one is enmeshed. 'If a man is making a positive attempt to extricate himself from or alter his situation he is not happy; the fact that we might judge him as ill-advised to alter what we regard as a favourable situation is of course neither here nor there, even if he later implicitly endorses our judgement.'[27]

5.19 Finally we have to answer the question of how we are going to explain such locutions as 'I think that I am happy', 'I don't know whether I'm happy' or 'I thought I was happy at the time, but I now see that I was mistaken'. Do such remarks not indicate both that it is possible for the agent to be mistaken and that rejection is not an infallible guide, since what a man rejects today he may regret having rejected tomorrow? No, they do not. Many situations or factors could render the above remarks quite legitimate and intelligible without upsetting or invalidating the analysis of happiness given. I may say 'I think' rather than 'I know' because I do not have a clear concept of happiness, which is the case with most people: they literally do not know whether the state they are in counts as happiness, because they haven't a clear view of what happiness is. The positive denial of knowledge on the matter might be due to the problem of deciding whereabouts on the continuum one is: I know that I'm somewhere between suicide and ecstasy, but it is difficult to decide whether to count it as happiness or not. Or a similar problem may arise out of doubt about how to weigh my state of mind in respect of some aspects of my life against a different state of mind in respect of others: would a happily married man, currently frustrated at work, classify himself on balance as happy or not? He may reasonably say he doesn't know. Again, changes of mind are very often to be explained in terms of fluctuating expectations: 'At the time I thought I was in paradise, now I know that this is paradise'. That makes sense, and in everyday language that may become 'I thought I was happy, but this is real happiness'. However, given the nature of happiness, it may be that this latter formulation is strictly speaking illegitimate. The difference between the two statements is that in the former 'in paradise' puts the emphasis on the quality of the situation, about which mistakes can be made and minds changed. But happiness is the product of how one stands in relation to a situation, and that, though it can change, cannot falsify the past. This situation can turn out to be no paradise, indeed to have been no paradise, but that won't show that I didn't think it was paradise: it shows only that I won't think it is anymore or that I wouldn't be happy there now. The fact remains that I was.

The only way in which I can turn out to have been mistaken is if it transpires that I have been misapplying the word - an error that I may detect and subsequently be better placed to avoid as a result of sharpening my conception of happiness.

CHAPTER 6

The Empirical Claims Examined

6.1 Now that we have a clear understanding of what happiness is, a clear conception of what we are talking about, we are in a position to reconsider critically the empirical research cited in the first chapter. In general the analysis of the concept given is confirmed by the empirical research in the only way that it can be: things that ought to be true, given the meaning of the term, turn out to be true, while there are no findings that conflict with the logical consequences of the analysis. Thus all studies reveal high correlation between people's reported feelings of alienation, depression, anxiety and anomie on the one hand and unhappiness on the other, which is exactly what we would expect. Indeed any evidence to the contrary would suggest that different concepts of happiness were in play, since, as we have seen, it is logically impossible to be happy and alienated or happy and depressed in respect of the same area of one's life. (See above, esp. 5.9)

It is also important to recognise at the outset that, given what happiness is, any society wishing to take active steps to promote happiness in individuals will need to engineer a correlation between what is possible and what people expect. This could be a question of altering circumstances or people, or both. But however it is done, it is a matter of logic that to *control* one's happiness one needs realistic expectations.

6.2 Bailey, it may be recalled, maintains that our happiness is dependent on our ability to create and appreciate beauty, to take satisfaction in physical activity, to perform obligations of service and to find intellectual fulfilment (see above, ch. 1).[1] He clearly feels, although he is careful not to commit himself to this view, that 'an endless series of beers guzzled in front of the television set carrying an endless series of organised thuds and punitive bangs is not as much evidence of happiness as rich patrons sitting in their box seats watching Tristan and Isolde through pearl-covered opera glasses' (p. 42). And he does assert that in general we are the victims of 'the desensitising and dehumanising character of the diversions that pummel us' (p. 42).

Leaving aside the further question of whether it is true, and, if so, to what extent, that television desensitises us, there seems little or no evidence to support Bailey's overall contention. If you define happiness in terms of activity, as he does ('a felicitous inner condition achieved by activity'), then obviously it will have to be found in activity, though even then it does not follow that it must lie in the activities mentioned by him. Again, if happiness is a 'felicitous' condition of some sort, then of course *appreciation* of art, physical *satisfaction,* and intellectual *fulfilment* are going to be possible (although not necessarily necessary) source of happiness: any kind of appreciation, satisfaction or fulfilment will contribute to happiness. But in any case (as the argument shows in chapter 5) there seems no good reason to accept this limited definition of happiness, which so obviously begs half the questions. All in all there seems to be nothing to support either the odd touch of rhetoric about freedom being necessary for happiness or the specific assertion that happiness can, and can only, derive from the four sources mentioned.

What may very well be true is that 'the complexity and rarity' in the aesthetic domain permits a 'truly rich and lasting aesthetic satisfaction' and that we have in the contemplation of nature itself a potential source of enormous satisfaction (p. 43). But the claim that certain pursuits may as a matter of fact lead to great happiness is quite different from the claim that happiness is logically or necessarily tied to them. There is all the difference in the world between asserting that popular music cannot lead to real happiness in a way that classical music can, and saying 'What does seem clear . . . is that those experiences . . . that leave a legacy of longer term satisfaction . . . tend to be those that have have been "worked at", where literally "pains" have been taken' (p. 44). If this latter claim were empirically proven, that would provide the beginning of a good case for 'appropriate educational preparation' so that people could find happiness through such things as love of the arts – not on the unwarranted grounds that ballet appreciation contributes to true happiness while enthusiasm for pop music does not, but on the grounds that the former as a matter of fact provides a more sustained source of happiness. Whether the claim is true (or true of some people perhaps?) cannot be finally decided here. But it does seem prima facie plausible to suggest that, for those who are capable of appreciating both, complex activities should prove a more long-lived source of rich satisfaction than simple activities. This is not to say that people who appreciate only relatively simple activities must experience less satisfaction, or that such satisfaction and such activities are in themselves inferior. There might nonetheless be a case for introducing children to complex activities on the grounds that we cannot be sure in advance who is and who is not likely to be the kind of person capable of appreciating both kinds of activity and consequently likely to become dissatisfied with simple pursuits. It is incidentally more than likely that something of this sort was in Mill's mind when he tried to distinguish between pleasures on the grounds that those who were competent to judge (i.e. had experience of different kinds of pleasure) regarded the so-called higher pleasures as indeed superior to the lower pleasures. Mill cannot have meant that the higher pleasures were in themselves a qualitatively superior kind of pleasure, for that would contradict his view that pleasure is itself the sole criterion of value. But he could well have meant that the higher pleasures were better in that they were better *sources* of pleasure, being more reliable and more enduring.

Considerably more suspect is Bailey's attempt to tie happiness to a sense of obligation and service. It may be true that 'even with the twentieth century's massive depreciation of Victorian rhetoric, millions of people have continued to find nourishment of the free self in the fulfilment of perceived obligations and in the performance of voluntary service' (p. 45). But millions of people have also nourished the free self in other ways, and we have been given no reason to regard this particular form of nourishment as a necessary source of happiness. It is possible that for some people, namely those whose character is such that they feel the need to carry out such obligations, this should prove a sufficient source of happiness, but then there is no necessary reason why there should be people of such a character in the first place. In exactly the same way, although it may be true, at least for some people, that 'few human experiences can match in sheer exhilaration the rewards of the cultivated mind at play and at work along the frontiers of its capacity' (p. 46), it is certainly not the only way, a necessary way or, I should imagine, in itself a guaranteed way to happiness.

Bailey's position is important in that it embodies a quite common view among educationalists that happiness is inextricably bound up with the serious and the good. But, although there may be a case for saying that throughout history certain activities have proved capable of providing a rich and reliable source of happiness, and although one might go further and build on the idea of complexity being connected with a potentiality for sustained enjoyment, we must still face up to the fact that no case has been presented for limiting the possible sources of happiness in any way, least of all by reference to Bailey's particular candidates. Given what happiness is, there is no necessary reason why one should not find it as well in combing one's hair all day as in composing or listening to Mahler's symphonies.

6.3 The hint of standard rhetoric on freedom to be detected in Bailey is the dominant note in Ervin and is to be stoutly resisted, for it is clear that there are neither logical nor empirical grounds for insisting that happiness depends upon freedom. Ervin's thesis is that economic, personal, political, intellectual and religious freedom are essential to allow man to pursue happiness.

> Man has many needs and many longings. As a physical being he has material necessities and cravings. As an individual being, he wants to enjoy dignity and respect. As a political being he desires a voice in government and freedom from tyranny. As an intellectual being he wishes to use his mind freely. As a spiritual being, he longs to bow his own knees before his own god in his own way.[2]

All of these may, perhaps, represent very laudable objectives. They may be true statements as contingent generalisations about contemporary Americans. But they are not in any way a binding or compelling prescription for happiness. The pursuit of happiness is *not necessarily* 'the quest for satisfaction of these needs and longings'. Only for those people who happen to have such needs and longings could it be true that happiness lies in that quest, and there is no law of human nature that says anybody must have them. Equally suspect are Scheiser's view that the collectivist totalitarian tendency of the organisation of most schools (itself a tendentious description) must be anti-happiness and Neill's complementary view that people can only be happy in an unstructured free setting.[3] The truth is rather (as Plato well saw, since it is partly a matter of logic and arises out of the fact that happiness is a sense of enmeshment or harmony, as psychologists such as Erich Fromm have appreciated, and as empirical studies such as those of Bronfenbrenner and Hsu confirm) that totalitarian societies are just as likely in practice (and more so in theory) to promote happiness. (Hsu found less *extremes* of either misery or happiness, but more enmeshment, which is happiness, in social-centred China than in individual-centred America.)[4]

All the evidence (empirical and reasoning) suggests that the connection between happiness and freedom is of the sort supposed by Mill in his essay *On Liberty*,[5] (properly understood). Mill, while, consistently with his avowed utilitarian position, seeing the principle of utility or the maximisation of happiness as the supreme consideration, nonetheless valued freedom highly. But he did not value it because he believed that free men must necessarily experience more present happiness than unfree men. He valued it (in so far as, and in the ways that, he did) because he believed that in the long run the freedom would lead to the development and control over life that would make mankind the gainers in terms of happiness.

6.4 Butler is evidently correct in observing that the pursuit of happiness is to be distinguished from 'the egocentric and ethnocentric satisfaction of greed and pleasure',[6] even though it could be the case that some individuals would find their happiness (a sense of enmeshment) by such means. He is also correct, as other evidence has shown,[7] in stressing the importance of a sense of belonging to family, peer group, community and country in respect of happiness. The explanation of this lies not in a direct contingent relationship between things like family life and happiness, but in the fact that a sense of belonging (to anything) is conceptually related to happiness, inasmuch as a sense of not belonging, a sense of alienation, is logically incompatible with happiness. Given that, and given the contingent facts of our social organisation, it is not surprising that for most of us a sense of belonging to the particular groups mentioned should be important. One positive step, therefore, that we might take in the interests of happiness, would be the development in people of a sense of belonging.

Butler goes on to suggest several more; he concludes with a summary of an eight-point plan for government action in the interests of the happiness of society generally. First, he argues, human benefit should be put before such considerations as economic profit or technological advancement, in planning and political action. Second, the 'happiness of mankind should encompass responsibility to individual merit and to an ideal of excellence coupled with full opportunity from the beginning of life for persons to grow into disciplines of personal achievement and satisfaction'.[8] Third, we should be concerned about 'keeping open the avenues and universalising the opportunities for every person' so as to give them 'adequate opportunity for self-realisation'. Fourth, we should encourage 'participatory democracy'. Fifth, hypocrisies and paradox should be eradicated from our institutions and faith in them revitalised. Sixth, we should stop permitting 'economically motivated acquisitiveness to define' what justifies 'institutional and systematic inhumanity'. Seventh, the nation should seek to be 'a shining light and a model of principle' that converts its affluence 'into altruistic purpose', and, finally, we should learn to live charitably together.

Unfortunately, like a fair amount of the writing on happiness, when the above is closely examined in the light of a clear conception of happiness, much of it seems to crumble into a heap of rhetoric and pious platitude. The first suggestion seems slightly simplistic. After all, there are occasions on which human benefit and economic profit might coincide. If Butler means that where they clash human benefit should come first, there is a danger that his advice is mere tautology: in recommending that for the sake of happiness we should put human benefit first, he might be saying no more than 'put happiness first', since human benefit is very often understood as being one with human happiness, particularly when it is contrasted with economic benefit. There is more than a hint of tautology in the second proposal too, since it is a matter of definition that happiness should involve satisfaction of some sort; beyond that, however, there seems no particular warrant for the intrusion of values specifically pertaining to the American ideal. It is by no means clear that any stress on individual merit is necessary for people's happiness. What is important is that whatever is classified as meritorious by a given society should be an object of respect for all individuals, because otherwise there will be a lack of enmeshment between what they want to see and what they do see around them. Again, the third and fourth suggestions unwarrantably try to impose certain specific American values, which, at best, are only important to the happiness of those who do now hold to the American ideal. The fifth demand, on the other hand, is surely correct and culture free. People's happiness must be diminished to the extent that they see hypocrisy (whether it is actually there or not) in institutions that dominate their society. The sixth point seems hardly to add to the first, while the seventh and eighth seem merely rhetorical flourishes.

Nonetheless, if we simplify and extract, Butler is surely correct to assert that in order to promote happiness we need to promote a sense of togetherness and corporate identity, a degree of belief in our way of life (whatever it may be), and very possibly we would be well advised to put happiness up front publicly, so that people come to feel no embarrassment in doing things just for the sake of happiness.

6.5 Other detailed claims about sources and conditions of happiness can be dealt with more summarily. The view that children's happiness 'comes as they begin to make and remake choices and commitments'[9] surely unwarrantably asserts a logical connection between choice and happiness, as Russell too tries to maintain there is (3.7). It is true that the question of happiness or lack of it cannot arise until the stage at which the child has the requisite consciousness to recognise things as alterable and conceivably different. But any connection between happiness and choice in a more usual sense is purely contingent, even within an open society that allows of and expects a great deal of choice. There may, on the other hand, be something in the idea that in pursuing happiness there 'is no substitute for being in touch with guides who are themselves conscious of and actively engaged in the pursuit'.[10] At any rate, though looking for happiness may not be the best way to secure it (see below 8.9), being surrounded by people who openly value and welcome happiness must be more likely to cause one to enjoy it than would being surrounded by people who seem to fear or be embarrassed by it. Perhaps happiness is caught rather than taught, at least to the extent that the assumption that all is for the best in the best of all possible worlds is infectious, and a cheerful disposition may be as much the product of environment as anything else.

Davidson's view that 'a sense of responsibility rather than hedonism is necessary for the elusive goal of happiness'[11] involves a false antithesis: there is no necessary incompatability between a sense of responsibility and the search for pleasure. One suspects that the view also involves wishful thinking: what evidence is there that those with a developed sense of responsibility are happier than those without? What conceptual connection is there between the two? A hedonist, if that means a person who seeks his own pleasure, may be as responsible as anyone else. Schieser's related view that more 'personalising' in education would increase happiness we have already questioned (6.3). Jokeil's finding that there is no significant correlation between happiness and success is entirely to be expected given that success was conceptualised in the research in objective terms (see above, 1.6).[12] In other words what the research confirms is what has already been asserted as a matter of logic: being well paid, being at the top of one's profession, being respected as a prominent figure and such like do not necessarily bring happiness. Similarly Anne Constantinople's finding[13] that the level of happiness amongst college students is closely associated with a basic trust and a sense of identity (as measured on the Inventory of Psycho-social development) is to be expected: to lack trust and to feel isolated are two dimensions of lacking a sense of enmeshment.

There is, finally, a mass of not very satisfactory or conclusive research that suggests that academic success, money, sex, love, relations with parents, job prospects and value conflicts are amongst the most important factors that contribute to happiness or lack of it for students. Such research is unsatisfactory because of its inherent difficulties. Kramer, for example, comes up with the finding that most of his sample regarded their choice of job as more of a problem than their personal unhappiness, which seems exceedingly curious since one would have thought that the latter encompassed the former.[14] ('I'd rather have my job settled than be happy' seems very odd.) Some wish to draw the conclusion from this research that

Houston is wrong to claim that 'academic aspects of student life are causing the most stress',[15] but it is difficult to be sure of that or any other conclusion, since one does not know to what extent members of Kramer's sample linked and submerged their academic fears under alternative headings like 'vocational', 'career-planning' or indeed the general category 'personal unhappiness'. One thing that is certain is this: any attempt to draw up a plan of action on the basis of such research, that involved minimising tension about whatever items seem to head the list as putative sources of unhappiness, would quite miss the point of the nature of happiness and the shortcomings of such research. In the first place it is quite wrong to interpret the most frequently cited source of unhappiness as necessarily the most damaging; in the second place as soon as source *X* is resolved it is, as often as not, replaced by source *Y* and there is no necessary diminution of unhappiness; in the third place happiness is acquired not by removing sources of tension but by coming to grips with them so that they do not induce tension. A man is not happy because he thinks he is safe from various threats and anxieties; he is happy when he does not recognise threats and anxieties.

The high correlation that has been noted more than once between happiness and self-esteem is to be expected, since the notion of someone who has a low opinion of himself and yet a sense of enmeshment is incoherent. Thus Landry's research (1.6) showing that individuals whose scores significantly differ at different times in respect of self-concepts show corresponding variations on the factor scales of happiness is predictable.[16] This points to one line of action that could be taken to promote happiness – namely, enhance the individual's self-concept. Strong's Unself programme (1.4)[17] has some relevance here, for, although there can be no warrant for the assumption that to be less self-centred is necessarily to be happier, it may be the case that self-centred happiness is more precarious for the individual (and less beneficial to others). MacLeod's[18] thesis that creativity and happiness are linked (1.4) seems trite and contrived. Citing the case of Van Gogh, he himself admits that creative talents are not sufficient to ensure happiness, and they are obviously not necessary. Furthermore, creativity as it is normally understood, whether in the context of great art, great science or the three-year-old expressing himself spontaneously, does not mean what MacLeod makes the word mean. For him a creative person is one who is 'able to come up with more good ideas for solving problems' (p. 227) than others. Given that definition, it can be argued that, if the world is problematic, the creative will be less upset by it. But such redefinitions tell us nothing about the real world, and certainly do not show that by developing creativity in any normal sense of the word we are enhancing the individual's chances of happiness.

Many studies have shown 'a significant correlation between life satisfaction and church attendance and church related activity'[19] (though, before rushing to instil religion in the cause of happiness, we should note that Mathiasen found that 'church activity at age 12 had no significance relatively to present church attendance' amongst a sample of elderly people in the Bible Belt area of America[20]). What is particularly interesting, however, and rather unexpected, is that it is participation in religious activities rather than a religious attitude that is 'significantly related to happiness'.[21] This is unexpected because. whereas there seems no immediate reason to connect activities such as church attendance with happiness, religious faith (implying here belief in a benevolent and omnipotent overseer) would seem certain to enhance one's sense of all being well with the world. But perhaps this distinction between religious acts and religious attitudes is itself a bit suspect: it is certainly difficult to conceive of many people who would be able and willing to say of themselves that they freely participated in religious activity without religious beliefs. What is clear is that those who have a faith (of any sort) must thereby gain a degree of that sense of enmeshment that constitutes happiness.

6.6 It would be as well to remind ourselves that the attitudinal research needs to be handled even more cautiously than other research relating to a concept like happiness. The dangers and the uses of such research have been well summarised by Lazarsfeld in his expository review of *The American Soldier*,[22] an intensive study of the soldier's life during the Second World War, which was largely based on studies of people's expressed attitudes. The limitations of such 'survey methods are obvious', writes Lazarsfeld. 'They do not use experimental techniques; they rely primarily on what people say, and rarely include objective observations; they deal with aggregates of individuals rather than with integrated communities; they are restricted to contemporary problems'(p. 378). More obviously still, one might add, they presuppose clear conceptions and shared meanings of words, which in point of fact are most unusual, and they presuppose in people a degree of insight and impartial self-scrutiny that is generally lacking. On the other hand

> the findings of regularities is the beginning of any science, and surveys can make an important contribution in this respect . . . it is necessary that we know what people usually do under many and different circumstances if we are to develop theories explaining their behavior . . . before we can devise an experiment we must know what problems are worthwhile.[p. 379]

The defence is cogent so far as it goes, though in ignoring the issue of whether the surveys are not intrinsically suspect it may be said that it doesn't go very far. But certainly Lazarsfeld has the last laugh in the splendid passage where he leads the reader to assert of half a dozen findings that 'of course they were only to be expected', only to reveal subsequently that the very reverse was actually found in each case.

Some of the broader findings of the research to which Lazarsfeld refers are relevant to this enquiry — for example, the conclusion that attitudes of individuals are influenced by their expectations, the phenomenon of relative deprivation and evidence about the disconcerting affects of uncertainty. Of particular interest is the finding that the primary groupings of social life, such as family and work groups, shape individuals' attitudes and provide emotional support to a great extent, and that anxiety is experienced when contact with the primary group is lost. As with other similar research such conclusions must not be interpreted to mean that the family group is logically necessary to happiness, but it does suggest that within our culture there is a contingent connection. That was also the finding of the Institute for Social Research. Two studies from that source[23] show that 'marriage and family life are the most satisfying parts of most people's lives and being married is one of the most important determinants of being satisfied with life' (p. 3). Other points to emerge from these studies include the claim that 'satisfaction is additive' in the sense that 'the more satisfaction in any of a dozen or so domains, the greater the overall feeling of contentment' (p. 4), and the claim that certain domains, specifically health, marriage, job and income 'carry a little more weight than others'. (But the tentative nature of this sort of research is illustrated by the fact that other reports suggest that marriage is not a significant domain and that health is of significance as a source of fears rather than as a source of hopes.[24]) Note also that 'despite the conviction of many social observers that women *ought* to feel more frustrated and unrewarded than men, the bulk of the evidence from these studies is that they do not'.[25] The housework does not appear to cast a pall over the life of the housewife, except that 'college graduate women who are housewives find their lives less rewarding than other housewives and in particular less rewarding than the lives of college graduate women who are employed'.[26] This finding is of course grist to the analysis of happiness given, for it is just what we should have predicted: happiness, being a sense of enmeshment, depends upon matching expectations and reality, and has nothing to do with what observers would like to see or think is desirable. (This point is borne out by the research of *The American Soldier* too.) Most women are happy as housewives because most women have grown up to cast their expectations in that mould; college graduates, by contrast, are likely to have other ambitions and to see the role of the housewife as inhibiting. Consequently the latter tend to find the role of housewife frustrating.

6.7 The most prominent correlations revealed by attitudinal research are unsurprising because they are clearly conceptual connections. (Self-esteem, social adjustment and successful involvement with others, if contrasted with unsuccessful involvement rather than non-involvement, *should* correlate with happiness, because of the meanings of the terms involved.) The evidence that good personal relationships, economic well-being, high status and the converger mentality tend to lead to happiness is less tautologous and more interesting. Presumably the importance of the first three as sources of happiness is the result of the importance attaching to social life, money and fame or repute in our society, while convergers tend to find happiness because, by definition, they frame their expectations in the light of the current norms and habits of society.

That people find family circumstances a source of hopes and the international situation a source of fears is interesting. Perhaps it can be adequately explained in this way: a healthy international situation does not affect the private individual as obviously and directly as an unhealthy one does. To put it at its most extreme:

with universal peace and goodwill between nations, the private individual may still live a tiresome daily life. With widespread war and destruction he will find it difficult to pursue a strictly private life. Conversely, if we assume some typical degree of concern on the part of an individual for his family, it is not difficult to understand that their joys should materially increase his happiness.

It is not at all surprising that there should be a significant correlation between incapability and discontent: by and large one is aware of one's incapability and it is that awareness, the perception that one fails and cannot achieve what one would like to do, that destroys one's sense of enmeshment rather than incapability itself. The evidence does not show, and I should be very surprised if it did, that failure as such is necessarily a cause of unhappiness; one would expect the extent to which failure in itself does cause unhappiness to vary in accordance with society's attitude to failure. On the other hand, that overachievers are happy is surely a matter that owes more to logic than society's attitudes. An overachiever is, by definition, one who does better than he had thought he would or had been led to expect he could do – there cannot, consequently, be any significant lack of fit between the overachiever's expectations and the realisation of those expectations. In much the same way the mass of evidence relating to job satisfaction both confirms and further elucidates the analysis of happiness given. The finding that, in the interests of job satisfaction, intelligence should be neither too high nor too low for the job in question accords both with commonsense and with the view that happiness involves an equilibrium between person and situation or between outlook and opportunity. Indeed the wording of the conclusion of a report on such research reads like an analysis itself: 'job satisfaction is probably the result of interactive influence of personality and environmental factors.'[27]

W. Wilson's summary of the features or characteristics of the happy man (1.6) can now be seen to be more than probable and convincing, a large part of it being essentially analytic.[28] One would be surprised indeed if it turned out that the happy man need not be optimistic, worry-free, possessed of self-esteem or of good morale in respect of his job. Less obviously, but no less truly, one would expect modest aspirations to lead to happiness, since they are more likely to be fulfilled. As we have seen, there is no reason to suppose that religion is necessary to happiness, but every reason to believe that religion, providing, as it does, a faith and a way of life that bring together outlook and reality, would tend to be a source of happiness. That the happy are usually young, healthy and well-paid must surely be contingent, but not particularly unexpected given the way we are; that the happy person may be of either sex and a wide range of intelligence is welcome news, and again hardly amazing. Perhaps the only real surprise thrown up by this summary of the research is the intimation that happy people tend to be well-educated and extrovert. For that there seems no immediate logical or empirical explanation, and, in default of such, I would be inclined to suppose that it is the fact that in our society such factors may well increase social mobility and bring in their train satisfying jobs, money, status and an absence of worry that explains their appearance as factors contributing to happiness. (Below I shall suggest a more direct link between education and happiness — 8.9.)

6.8 The questions of why people continue to be unhappy, why indeed, as appears to be the case, they are increasingly unhappy, and of what might be done about it must now be raised. The answer is very simple and has been well summarised by Rescher.[29] Increased physical or material well-being does not and has not brought increased happiness because 'an individual's assessment of his happiness is a matter of his personal and idiosyncratic perception of the extent to which the conditions and circumstances of his life meet his needs and aspirations' (p. 95). In other words, the circumstances in which we are placed are not only not necessarily going to make us happy — they cannot be sufficient. We have to have a match between attitude and circumstance. It turns out that Epicurus was as near the mark as anyone with his contention that degree of satisfaction equals one's attainment divided by one's expectation. That is borne out by both analysis and empirical research. 'What we are facing [in contemporary society] is an escalation of expectations, a raising of the levels of expectation, with corresponding increased aspiration in the demands people make upon the circumstances and conditions of their lives' (p. 96). This explains why material prosperity does not necessarily bring increased happiness, and in this case has not. It also explains, what might otherwise seem inexplicable, that people can and do sincerely believe past ages to have been happier than our own, and yet do not wish to revert to those times themselves. People — *those* people, with *their* outlook — were happier than we are now; that does not mean that *we*, with our outlook, would also have been happier. Rescher's conclusion is that to increase happiness we need to reduce available means and thereby reduce expectations. The principle is obviously correct (although it does not necessarily have to be done by reducing the so-called quality of life); the only overall way to increase happiness is to meet or reduce expectations.

Whether we should attempt to meet or reduce expectations, and, if so, what we might do in specific terms will be considered in the last two chapters. Here it is enough to dwell upon the point that everything points to this conclusion: if we want to increase happiness, by some means or other we *must* meet or reduce expectations. There are of course a number of things we might do immediately to lessen unhappiness here and there, to a greater or lesser extent. Alienation from social norms is clearly one source of unhappiness; poverty another. But to concentrate on offsetting the consequences of particular sources of unhappiness such as these is only scratching the surface of the problem and only works in respect of particular individuals, if the world is otherwise unchanged. For as we become different people we both develop new expectations and create a new situation that requires a different kind of response. I take none of the delight in torture that my ancestors did; nor do you and there is consequently little of it about. But removing that source of misery has not led to any overall increase in happiness. Our minds are set on different things. The threat of torture is replaced by the threat of something else.

There is nothing for it but to juggle wholesale with both sides of the equation: expectations and actualities.

6.9 Finally, the question of drugs in relation to happiness deserves a section to itself. Jean Austin, it may be recalled, denied that a man high on drugs could be happy (see above, 1.6). It has already been conceded (5.17) that to seek happiness through drugs may be self-defeating in the long run. The question remains as to what precisely drugs can do and whether what they do deserves the name of happiness. There certainly are drugs, such as tricyclamines, that, even if they 'do not produce euphoria . . . do ameliorate depressive states' and Evans forewarns us of more ambitious things to come.[30]

There are also some experiments with epinephrene to be taken into account: Schacter and Singer's research[31] clearly shows (a) that certain bodily reactions, including crude sensations or feelings, can be artificially induced, and (b) that the subject's understanding or classification of such reactions is at least partly dependent on what he believes to be going on: palpitations can be induced that the subject may variously interpret as anger, happiness or something else, depending on how he interprets the situation. (How he does interpret the situation can be controlled and modified by such strategies as placing him in the company of others who appear to be enjoying themselves, who seek to irritate the subject, etc.)

Drugs such as tricyclamines would seem to make a contribution to happiness. A drug like epinephrene seems to be capable of causing symptoms typically, but not always and not only, associated with happiness. Happiness is a sense of enmeshment and as such must involve consciousness in the sense explained above. Tricyclamines create a particular state of consciousness. Epinephrene, by contrast, appears to create bodily states that have no meaning in isolation. The former engineer a change of attitude that increases enmeshment; the latter does not. There seems no doubt, then, that some drugs may properly be said to contribute to happiness. The reluctance of people like Jean Austin to accept this must be put down, and may plausibly be put down, to a feeling that such happiness is of questionable worth. So indeed it may be for various reasons: it may not be very thrilling; it may be bought at the price of a loss of autonomy; it may betoken deep sadness prior to taking drugs; it may be precarious or shortlived. It remains a species of happiness for all that. And the argument and the evidence are both important, for it seems that 'the faith held by psychopharmacologists that a person's mood and his neurochemical state were equivalent terms from different viewpoints seems to be on the road to justification'.[32]In the long run, it may be that happiness will prove more manageable than we had anticipated.

Also worth drawing attention to are Pitcher's examination of the awfulness of pain and Puccetti's examination of the sensation of pleasure.[33] Whether pleasure and happiness can be identified or not, pain is clearly antithetical to happiness. But, suggests Pitcher, one can experience pain that is not unpleasant: masochism, post-lobotomy experience ('typically these patients report that they still have pain but it doesn't bother them; they simply no longer care about the pain and often forget it is there' – p. 482[34]), and fakirs all seem to testify to the possibility of taking pleasure in painful stimuli. Some might feel that in such cases the awfulness of pain is merely overriden by some other consideration or, perhaps, cancelled out. Others will argue that real pain is experienced and enjoyed in such contexts. Pitcher sees no way to resolve that debate, but suggests that all parties have hitherto assumed that what, say, the masochist feels is *pain.* He then refers to research[35] that suggests that visceral responses, such as the rate of heartbeat, can be controlled by the subject: 'the brain is capable of controlling things that happen in the body . . . This suggests the possibility that perhaps the brain is able to act in such a way as to alter the intensity of a sensory signal that would otherwise reach the brain' (p. 487). In other words the dog's brain (dogs were the subject of this research by Melzack and Wall) may not be stimulated by the usual signal - it may not, so to speak, *get* the pain! What is posited here is a form of gate-control and Pitcher suggests that anxiety might serve to open the gate, while indifference about some matter might serve to keep it closed. Such a system would explain such phenomena as the fact that some women experience pain in pregnancy and childbirth and others do not. At present perhaps little can be made of Pitcher's theorising, since, as Noren and Davis point out,[36] nothing is said about how or why the gate is closed, even assuming that it is, when, for example, people are indifferent about something. Noren and Davis are right to distinguish the philosophical and empirical elements in this thesis, however, and what may be of significance here and now are the Melzack and Wall findings to the effect that, in so far as normally painful stimuli can be controlled, we have a tangential aid to happiness.

Puccetti refers to Olds' discovery that a stimulus to the rhinencephalon seems to please rats to the extent that they willingly forgo food for the sake of it.[37] Further experiment suggested that about 60 per cent of the rat brain is motivationally neutral and some 5 per cent of the implantation sites produce avoidance reactions; but the rhinencephalon turns out to be 'a relatively low inducement' area when stimulated compared to, say, the posterior hypothalmus, which, implanted with electrodes, could cause the rat to press the bar that activates the sensation as much as 5000 times an hour. 'If . . . a rat in a Skinner box chooses to pump the treadle 5,000 or 7,000 times an hour, shunning normal organic satisfactions or even accepting pain to do it, surely he is getting *something* in return. What is this, if not pleasure?' (p. 241).

Puccetti's main point is that this research throws considerable doubt on some philosophical accounts of pleasure that deny that it is a sensation on the grounds that it is inseparable from its source, neither a cause nor an effect and not something locatable or clockable. To Olds' research findings he adds reference to Lilly's work with monkeys that suggests that physical decline caused by pain can be cancelled out by artificial stimulation of pleasure centres, which suggests that pleasure is a sensation comparable to pain – a point that has been denied by some philosophers. 'From a miserable, dying organism he [monkey] is transformed, literally within minutes, into a healthy, responsive one. It is as if he had never been sick at all. Nature seems to have placed rats and monkeys, at least, under the governance of those sovereign masters, pleasure and pain' (p. 243). Limited research with human beings suggests that similar findings might be encountered with them.

Alan Fuchs[38] has challenged Puccetti both on his interpretation of some of the data and on the issue of whether this research invalidates what certain philosophers have said. He reports, for example, that in one set of experiments a 'patient continued to press a button that was supposedly stimulating his brain for 2,000 times after the stimulating current was turned off' (p. 500). He also suggests that Puccetti has misunderstood the nature of the philosophical problem and that the evidence cited actually supports the view that pleasure is not a sensation! For our present purposes that particular issue is not as important as the undoubted fact that people can be artificially stimulated to want to repeat even aimless and trivial activities.

But is that happiness or contributory to it? I would be inclined to suggest a difference between a drug-induced outlook (which might involve a pleasurable state of mind that can be regarded as constitutive of happiness) and a neuro-physically located feeling (which involves a sensation of pleasure that might contribute to happiness, but is not a constitutive part of it). The latter might be compared to sexual pleasure or the pleasure of inhaling cigarette smoke – possible sources of happiness, but not constituent parts of it.

These are evidently early days for this area of research but, even if it is correct to withstand the suggestion that electrodes convey happiness, it does seem reasonable to cast aside the traditional view that happiness is something above and beyond the control of the scientist. The use of the soma of *Brave New World* may be repugnant to us in some ways, but the day may be coming when it will be possible to increase happiness by means of it – and happiness will be the right word for it.

CHAPTER 7

The Value of Happiness

7.1 It is important to distinguish between criticisms of the propriety or logical possibility of pursuing happiness on the one hand and practical difficulties that may hinder us while, or prevent us from, pursuing happiness on the other. There are obviously many, many problems that we would run up against in practice, if our object was to promote people's happiness far and wide. But here I want to concentrate on the other question – thrown into relief by the implications of some of the neurophysical evidence – namely, the question of the proper limits that should be set around the pursuit of happiness. In the light of all that has so far been said we have to take stock and ask is happiness important, ought we to be concerned to promote it, if so should schooling play a part and, if so, what part? Is there, in short, sufficient value in happiness to make it worth our attention, either generally or specifically as educationalists?

As we have seen there is no doubt that as a matter of fact people think that happiness matters. D.C. Butler's research led to the conclusion that students, the general public and educators alike all placed happiness high, sometimes highest, on their list of desired ends.[1] This finding is supported by other research such as that of Blai,[2] whose study of Harcum Junior College showed that all students regarded happiness as their most important goal, and the 'Mood of American Youth' survey, which found that 'happiness and family life are valued as vital elements to a complete and satisfying life'.[3] There is more than a smack of tautology about that remark, of course (how could one have a complete and satisfying life while being unhappy?); nonetheless the spirit of it has never been seriously challenged by research. Happiness is generally thought to be a good thing.

Switching direction slightly we may note that most people would argue that it is a matter of logic rather than contingency that people do value happiness, because it would be more or less unintelligible to deny that it had any worth. Thus Dearden writes

> surely it is the case that a man cannot be said to have understood what happiness is if he does not see in the fact that something would promote or contribute to his happiness *a* reason for action . . . To have understood what happiness and pleasure are is at least to have seen that we cannot be called upon to justify the pursuit of them, other things being equal.[4]

Dearden goes on to endorse Aristotle's point that happiness is, furthermore, the only end that is always chosen for its own sake alone. Friendship, money or fame might be regarded as ends in themselves, but they could be pursued as means to something else (including one another and happiness). I might desire friends for the sake of happiness, or money for the sake of fame, or fame for the sake of friends I think it will bring me. But happiness is never chosen as a means: I could not want happiness for the sake of money, fame, friendship or anything else.

We may now assert categorically that happiness is an end and cannot be valued as a means to some other end. 'Happiness is something I am not fond of' is incomprehensible, essentially because it would amount to saying 'I like to feel out of tune or at odds with my circumstances; I welcome anxiety, depression, alienation, etc.', which would be absurd. It may be possible to choose to forgo this end at particular times ('I must lay aside considerations of my own happiness'), but it is not possible to see happiness as inherently worthless or to see it only as a means to something else of more worth.

7.2 However, to establish that happiness is an end, both empirically and logically, is not the same thing as showing that it is the only or even the supreme end. It does not seem that people always value happiness alone or even more than a variety of other ends; at any rate they frequently say that they value other ends equally or more than happiness. At this point we must therefore raise the question of whether that kind of claim is logically coherent.

For it has often been argued that it is a matter of logical necessity that happiness should always be pursued.

It might be said, quite simply, that whatever people do when they have freedom of action (whatever they choose to do) is what they want to do, and that, since what they want to do is what brings them happiness, they evidently pursue happiness whenever they can. Obviously, it may be said, if I choose to marry, I want to marry; if I want to marry, presumably that is because I think that I will be happy when married. The argument does not of course suggest that one always imagines one will be extremely happy or that one's assumption about one's future happiness will always turn out to have been well-founded. It only suggests that, of the available courses of action open to you at a given time, you will do that which you think promises most happiness. But it seems an unsatisfactory argument anyway. The only interpretation of it that would give it validity would also make it true by definition and rather empty. If we take 'being happy' to mean 'doing what you want to do', then it is obviously true that, whenever we can, we pursue happiness, but all we would be saying is that whenever you choose to do something, you are doing that which you most want to do of the options available at the time. But if we recall our analysis of happiness as a sense of enmeshment, then it does not appear to be true that we always choose to do what we think will enhance our happiness. People freely choose to make sacrifices, they put duty before pleasure and in various other ways are willing to forgo or minimise their chances of immediate enmeshment, as for example does the young girl who forgoes the chance of marriage to the man she loves in order to nurse an invalid parent. Such an example makes it quite clear that happiness is not the sole value to which man does or logically can subscribe. There are other recognisable ends that are sometimes treated as taking preference and put before happiness.

However, it is still possible to argue, and I think correctly, that although people may pursue other ends in the short term and although they may think that they can and do pursue other ends in the long term, the latter is in fact logically impossible. On this view happiness is not the sole end, but it is the supreme end or value in the sense that no other end can coherently be regarded as equally or more important in the long term. It is not denied that present sacrifices of happiness may be made, but what is denied is the logical coherence of a plan of life that deliberately ignores happiness or subordinates it to some other value. That such a plan of life would be inconceivable can be easily shown, provided that we bear in mind what is meant by happiness. The question is whether it is conceivable that, in so far as a person has a long-term plan for life, he should adopt one that he is aware gives him less sense of enmeshment than he might have had. The answer to that must surely be in the negative. Certainly I might forgo a marriage that I acknowledge would have brought me much happiness, but, if I freely choose to make that sacrifice, it must be because there is something about me that makes me think, in the circumstances as they are, that to get married would be more intolerable than not, everything considered and taking the long-term view (unless, that is, I am simply making an obvious present sacrifice for a long-term gain). How can we believe that a person who sincerely thought that forgoing his marriage would, all-told and in the long term, taking the kind of person he happens to be into account, make him more unhappy than getting married, might nonetheless fail to marry? We cannot; we must assume rather that people who seem not to pursue happiness are merely so constituted (perhaps with a strong sense of duty, religious convictions, cowardice, etc.) that what appears to be the obvious path to happiness would for them be a source of such things as guilt, remorse and shame. (Perhaps I should add that this is not to say that people must see the matter in these terms. People may, for example, see themselves as acting from a sense of duty. The point is that in so far as a sense of duty motivates them, it is, whether they consciously recognise it or not, bound up with their chances of enmeshment.)

The claim that I am here making is that, although it is certainly true that we may sacrifice present happiness for future happiness or for other values, that we may make mistakes and fail to secure happiness, that we may think we value other things more and that there are other values besides happiness, nonetheless, in so far as a man were to plan his whole life (including reference to an afterlife, if he believes in one) he must treat happiness as the supreme value. Taking the long-term view a man must aim for enmeshment, whether he appreciates the fact or not.

7.3 But if we have shown anything so far, we have only shown that people do want their own happiness rather than anything else.

How is it possible to move from that factual statement, to the ethical view that people's happiness in general ought to be promoted, which we need to do if we want to extract any prescriptions for conduct from this enquiry into happiness. Nothing follows automatically from the mere fact that people must ultimately want their happiness more than anything else, except that, in so far as they are able to, they will act accordingly. To draw conclusions of a practical sort we need to establish that we ought to promote happiness in some particular way.

The classic and crucial text on this matter is the fourth chapter of John Stuart Mill's essay on *Utilitarianism*, where he argues, in outline, as follows: 'The only proof capable of being given that an object is visible, is that people actually see it . . . in like manner . . . the sole evidence it is possible to produce that anything is desirable, is that people do actually desire it.'[5] Thus happiness is presented as one of the ends of conduct. The next requisite step is to show that people not only 'desire happiness, but that they never desire anything else'; this is done by arguing that when people seem to desire something else, such as virtue, it is merely that that thing has come to be 'a principal ingredient of the individual's conception of happiness'. Thus happiness is shown to be the supreme end. Finally Mill remarks that 'no reason why the general happiness is desirable' can be given 'except that each person . . . desires his own happiness . . . Each person's happiness is a good to that person, and the general happiness therefore a good to the aggregate of all persons.'

Not, it may be thought, much of an argument. And what there is of it has been subjected to intensive criticism over the years. Particularly common has been the objection that Mill equivocates over the ambiguity of desirable. 'Desirable' may mean either 'capable of being desired' or 'ought to be desired'. That a thing is seen establishes that it is visible (capable of being seen). That a thing is desired establishes that it is desirable in one sense (capable of being desired), but not that it ought to be desired or that it is a thing of worth. Mill's view that other apparent ends are merely ingredients of happiness has been hotly disputed (though endorsed above), and, finally, there has been much disagreement and doubt about what Mill meant by his claim that the general happiness is a good to the aggregate of all persons, whether it is true in some sense and, if so, whether it follows without further argument from the observation that each person's happiness is a good to him.

My own view, first put forward in *Plato, Utilitarianism and Education*[6] is that most of such argument is beside the point, since Mill is not trying to *prove* that happiness is the supreme end as much as to provide *reasons* or *considerations* that would, in a memorable phrase, cause the mind to assent to the truth of the proposition. Specifically I take him to be showing in the first step of the argument not that we ought to desire happiness, but that happiness is the kind of thing that we might be prepared to recognise as the supreme end, since we do desire it and it is the only thing that all men necessarily do desire. 'The only thing', I concluded, 'that will command universal assent as something that ought to be desired, is the only thing that has actual universal assent as being desirable in the non-moral sense, namely enmeshment and hence happiness' (p. 92). The senses, respectively, in which I think it true and false to say that man only desires happiness as an end, I have explained above. As to the final step of the argument, while it seems clear that it does not follow as a matter of logical necessity from the fact that we all want our own happiness that the greatest happiness of the greatest number should be sought, it nonetheless seems intuitively plausible to regard the provision of happiness for all as a laudable aim or ideal, given the premiss that each man wants his own.

But the most persuasive interpretation of Mill seems to me to be John Kleinig's painstakingly precise reading of the text.[7] He lays stress both on the title of the chapter in question ('of what sort of proof the principle of utility is susceptible') and on Mill's statement that his prime concern here is with the question of 'what ought to be required of this doctrine – what conditions it is requisite that the doctrine should fulfil – to make good its claims to be believed'. This stress reminds us that Mill is not, as is often supposed, trying to *give us* the considerations 'capable of determining' the intellect to assent to the doctrine, but rather to outline or adumbrate the sort of considerations that would have to be given. He is trying, not to show (whether in the sense of 'prove' or 'provide reasons to provoke assent') that happiness is desirable as an end, but to point out that we would first need to show that it is, then need to show that the general happiness is an end and, finally, that it alone is, and also to indicate the sort of considerations that would be needed to establish each one of these steps.

According to Kleinig, then, in step 1 Mill wants only to observe that in order to show that happiness is desirable (i.e. can be desired) as an end, you could not do much more than produce evidence that people *do* desire it as an end. Now what sort of considerations would need to be given to show that the general happiness is desirable as an end? Kleinig suggests that Mill's point here is that 'it would be convincing to suggest that the general happiness was desirable as an end only if each person desired his own happiness as an end'. Finally, Mill is to be taken to say, it could only be reasonable to suggest that happiness is the sole desirable end if people do not desire other things as ends. After a digression to meet the objection that people *seem* to desire other things as ends ('whatever is desired otherwise than as a means to some end beyond itself and ultimately to happiness, is desired as itself a part of happiness, and is not desired for itself until it has become so'), Mill gets back to the point, which is to stress that what needs to be shown in order to prove that the general happiness is the only thing desirable as an end is that 'human nature is so constituted as to desire nothing which is not either a part of happiness or a means to happiness', which, as he goes on to say, is a matter for empirical investigation. Mill's statement that it would be 'a physical and metaphysical impossibility' to desire anything 'except in proportion as the idea of it is pleasant' is interpreted by Kleinig to mean that as a matter of both physical and psychological fact, if we find something pleasant, we desire it for its own sake or as an end.

Whether Kleinig interprets Mill correctly or not, his argument here has its own force: men just are so constituted that they are only capable of adopting as final ends what seems to them pleasurable in the sense of welcome or contributing to enmeshment. Of course different people, being different, will have different specific ends in mind; but for each individual his selected ends are seen by him as ingredients in happiness.

7.4 The preceding two sections contain arguments that, in my view, are sufficient to establish the supremacy of happiness amongst moral values. But it is not my purpose in this essay to convince the reader of that truth. For our present purpose we may concede that there is much that remains unresolved. Nonetheless it may be agreed that there are some grounds for regarding happiness as the supreme end of individual freely chosen activity and for going on to suggest that in social terms, other things being equal, we should seek to promote the happiness of everybody. At any rate such a moral principle could be embraced without qualms by everybody, whatever his other moral beliefs, and it is far from clear that that is true of any other proposed moral injunction.

But even if we were to agree that the promotion of the general happiness was in itself an acceptable ideal, it is undeniable that in fact people continually experience what they see as conflicts of value. Whatever the logic of holding to other ends besides happiness, people do value things like truth-telling, freedom, material equality and autonomy, and they do see what they regard as clashes either between these values themselves or between one of them and happiness. I am not now referring to clashes between one person's interests and another's, but more general clashes between the interests of, say, freedom and happiness as such. What ought we to do in situations where considerations of freedom dictate one policy and considerations of happiness another? There are, as far as I can see, only three options open to one:

(1) We may adopt the pluralist stance. According to this view there are a number of final ends of equal weight. If they are truly of equal weight an obvious consequence is that in cases of a clash there is no *correct* way of deciding which principle should take priority. Note that there is no question of judgement (in the sense of reasoned assessment as opposed to mere guesswork) either, for the problem is not that we do not know how to determine which principle should take priority; the problem is that no principle should take priority. They are, *ex hypothesi,* of equal weight. No decision, be it to take care of freedom first or to take care of happiness, can be wrong. It quite literally does not matter what we do in such a case. That conclusion seems so alien to our everyday moral sentiment that some may consider it an argument against the pluralist stance. (It should perhaps be pointed out that any suggestion to the effect that one should work out which principle ought to have priority in this particular instance would involve discarding the pluralist standpoint. For pluralism states that these principles are of equal weight. Any argument to the effect that *X* ought to take precedence over *Y* here, either directly asserts the superiority of *X* over *Y* or invokes some other principle, *Z,* in the

light of which the subordinate principles of *X* and *Y* can be assessed.)

(2) Taking refuge from the pluralist position one might espouse the hierarchical view, according to which there are a number of moral principles, but not of equal weight. Putting such an ethical code into practice may prove easier than living by the strict demands of pluralism, and it will give rise to a more consistent pattern of behaviour. The problem, however, is to explain the hierarchical order of the principles and to justify the priorities in question.

(3) A species of the hierarchical view is the view that assumes one dominant value in the light of which all clashes of subordinate principles have to be interpreted and settled. Such is the utilitarian view referred to in the preceding section. It is certainly the most satisfactory view judged as a workable system, but that of course does not mean that it encapsulates the truth. As to that, if we remain unpersuaded by the sort of considerations raised above, there is nothing for it but intuitive adherence to whichever seems the most plausible of these three positions.

Once again, it is not my concern here to settle this matter. I doubt if it can be settled and we do not need it settled for our immediate purposes. Suffice it to say that on any view happiness will be granted to be of considerable importance and, if it is not certain that it should be treated as being of supreme importance, it is evident that there is no theory that would seek to maintain that it must always be subordinated to something else that has been established either. On the face of it the promotion of happiness is as near to a universally agreed good as we are likely to get. That makes happiness pretty important in a social context. One question remains: what has it got to do with education?

CHAPTER 8

Happiness, Schooling and Education

8.1 In the first chapter it was suggested that there was no conceptual connection between happiness and education, and nothing that has been said since inclines me to change that view. Education just is not about making people happy, however earnestly one might hope that people will be happy while being educated or as a result of being educated. It is true that if one regards happiness as extremely important or as the supreme goal in social terms, as, say, the utilitarians do, one will be inclined to assess the whole enterprise of education with respect to that goal. A utilitarian might reasonably argue that education should cease altogether, if he had reason to believe that the practice of education all-told made the community considerably more miserable than its discontinuation would do. A utilitarian too should, theoretically, be of the opinion that the value of what is taught in schools ultimately has to be assessed by reference to the criterion of maximising happiness.[1] But even a utilitarian would accept that the question of what education is supposed to be about is distinct from the question of whether at the end of the day we wish to practise it, and that the answer to the former question has nothing to do with happiness. Perhaps, then, Dearden is right to say that

> the extent to which happiness has apparently now become an overriding consideration in some schools is even alarming. The belief is apparently abroad that everything in the classroom should be easy and a pleasure, for teacher and child alike, and, if it is not, then necessarily something is wrong . . . children must be 'kept happy' at all costs.[2]

But it is important to appreciate that the belief to which Dearden refers is not a necessary consequence of valuing happiness highly – not even of regarding it as the supreme value. Commitment to the value of happiness does not commit one to a laissez-faire attitude to education or to an overriding preoccupation with smiles and enjoyment, for at least three good reasons. First, concern for happiness does not commit one to concern only for present happiness; indeed, inasmuch as there is likely to be potentially more happiness in the future for most children, such concern rather suggests an emphasis on the long term, and obviously concern for long-term happiness may often lead to regarding other things as more important than present enjoyment. Second, concern for happiness does not commit one to concern only for the happiness of the individual. If happiness is what matters to you – happiness in and of itself, as opposed to your happiness or this child's happiness or the happiness of that class – then some account must be taken of ways of getting people to find their own happiness while contributing to or, at the very least, allowing the happiness of others. Once again there is little reason to suppose that concentrating on present smiles in the classroom is sufficient or necessary, let alone the best way, to take steps towards that objective. Third, as I have said, education is not in itself about happiness.

Obviously, in so far as we do value happiness, we want to promote it rather than destroy it. Other things being equal, we should hope that teaching methods, organisation, curriculum content, personal relationships and daily activities will be conducive to happiness and enjoyable, just as we hope that something like football will bring pleasure to players and spectators. But still, education is no more to be defined in terms of happiness than is football. The essence of football is to win by getting the ball into the opponent's net while abiding by a specific network of rules. The essence of education is understanding of a many-faceted kind: that is so even for the utilitarian.

8.2 Yet, as we have seen, for anybody, happiness is a value (7.2). Provided that the educational process as such is not interfered with or thwarted, provided nothing is done to hinder learning or inhibit understanding, we surely should be concerned with the happiness of pupils, long-term and short-term, considered both as individuals and as citizens. In itself, enjoyable education is preferable to unenjoyable education, and an education that incidentally contributes to happiness is superior in itself to one that does not. Furthermore, schools are concerned with more than education: they carry in addition responsibilities for socialising and training, and it might well be argued that promoting happiness *is* a proper aim of such schooling, even granting that it cannot be, strictly speaking, an aim of education.

All of this means that there are four ways in which happiness may be an important consideration in the context of schools.

(1) First, while granting primacy to the business of education, we may want education to be a happy experience for students, other things being equal.

(2) Secondly, it is plausible to argue that where young children are concerned education is not the priority. However implausible it might be to suggest that where fifteen-year-olds are concerned what matters most is that they should enjoy themselves, such a view seems quite reasonable with five-year-olds, at any rate provided such enjoyment does not get in the way of other activities like learning to read. In other words the priorities would be reversed here: since people can learn to read while in a situation where their present happiness is of paramount concern at least as well as in any other situation, it seems prima facie plausible to argue that happiness is the aim at this stage, while objectives such as getting the child to read, however important, are subsidiary.

(3) Thirdly, it may be argued that one of the functions of schooling is to provide pupils with the wherewithal to find happiness for themselves in the future. (To say that this is seen as a function of schooling rather than education is not to preclude the possibility that some of the wherewithal referred to may be acquired through education.)

(4) Fourthly, it may be argued, and in any community known to me will be argued, at least tacitly, that another function of schooling is to lead and enable pupils to live in ways that enhance or contribute to rather than diminish or interfere with the happiness of others.

It is quite conceivable that some or other of these objectives may from time to time be in conflict with another: steps designed to increase the individual's chances for his own future happiness do not necessarily serve the purpose of promoting the general happiness. The individual's present happiness may sometimes be in conflict with what is desirable for the sake of his own long-term happiness. Such conflicts, however, do not alter the fact that all four objectives may reasonably be adopted by schools. (There is also the question of the happiness of teachers to be taken into account, although in what follows I shall set that aspect of the matter aside.[3])

8.3 Assuming agreement on the point that schools may have a legitimate interest in the promotion of happiness, we have next to consider the various ways in which that interest might be served. One way is the provision of education itself, which may be an indirect source of happiness to people. (Here I am making a factual claim rather than any conceptual claim about education and happiness.) It will be recalled that a surprising number of people attribute their unhappiness in life to a lack of education (1.7). Such people may of course be mistaken — they might have been equally unhappy even if well educated, or they might have been very happy in their present uneducated state had certain other features of their lives been different. But that is not really the point. Since happiness is logically tied up with how people see things, to a considerable extent their perceptions, even if they are false, are more important than reality.[4] So long as education (which in this context probably means something like successful academic schooling) is both a means to ends that people generally desire (such as well-paid jobs or respect from other people) and/or perceived to be worth having either for its own sake or for extrinsic ends, whether in fact it is or is not, for so long will lack of education be a source of unhappiness. That is why, in our society as it is broadly constituted at present, ensuring the provision of education to people is a contribution towards their happiness.

But such a step will not take us far, especially as an increase in educational success judged from the teacher's and the individual's standpoint does not necessarily bring an increase in the sort of rewards and gratifications education can bring to the individual. In some cases the unhappiness will remain the same, and the only thing that will be different is that something else, such as the system or the boss, will be blamed as the cause of unhappiness.

8.4 What the promotion of happiness is really all about is the fitting of square pegs into square holes, round pegs into round holes and so on through all existing shapes. It is about the matching of expectations and possibilities or correlation between the individual's outlook and the contours of his actual situation. It is about harmony: the harmony of the parts of the individual soul (reason, will and desire); harmony between the individual's aspirations and his achievements; and harmony between the satisfied desires of one man and those of his fellows. What this implies in turn is that there are three essential conditions of happiness – security, self-esteem and realism – and our general strategy must seek to promote these three things.

I do not mean security from or in respect of anything in particular, but an overall sense of security. Perhaps this may be best explained in negative terms as an absence of such things as anxiety and uncertainty. Therefore I do not necessarily imply anything about specific needs such as financial security or marital stability, although no doubt in many cases lack of financial security or a broken marriage would lead to a lack of the sense of security about which I am talking. The evidence would seem to suggest that this sense of security will be enhanced by the growth of strong ties of affection within primary groups (e.g. family, peer group), a stable environment in which the individual knows what is expected of him and is not subject to random and arbitrary responses to his behaviour, and some degree of commitment to the beliefs and way of life of the community (and sub-communities) in question (see above, 6.3, 6.5, 6.6).[5]

By self-esteem I mean a proper pride in one's own worth. Once again, this is not tied to any particular achievements or abilities, so it is not vulnerable to the loss or absence of any particular talents, such as those conventionally valued by a community. It is not to be confused with conceit, pride, vanity, complacency or even a sense of being blessed by fortune, but rather, again in negative terms, an absence of feelings of self-doubt, futility, vileness or inadequacy. It is close to confidence, but not the sort of confidence that arises out of a sense of superiority, even if the latter is merited. No man can be happy who despises himself or thinks of himself in abject terms. It seems intuitively plausible to suggest that, in general, self-esteem will be nurtured by encouragement, praise and support, provided that it remains honest and does not encourage a false idea of his powers and worth in the individual. It is a question, in other words, of putting emphasis on what is good or successful rather than harping on what is poor and unsuccessful, and not of indiscriminately praising what is in fact unpraiseworthy. It seems that there is evidence that systematised programmes designed to enhance the individual's self-concept can be efficacious (6.5), but there does not seem any reason to regard them as necessary or superior to more informal techniques and practices.

The most important of the three elements is probably realism, by which I mean an outlook on life that does not distort or fantasise, but has an accurate perception of how things *are,* what people *are* like, what *is* likely to happen and so on. It is through realism that we can most effortlessly reduce our expectations and hence avoid disappointment. Obviously realism should not be confused with cynicism or defeatism. There is no suggestion that one should give up and accept the conditions of life as they are, whatever they are. The point is rather that aspirations and estimates relating to change and rejection should be realistic. Broadly speaking realism is a product of knowledge and understanding. But it is a mistake to think that, since we are talking of a realistic outlook on life, it is necessarily best acquired or exclusively acquired through experience of life. The nature of one's experience of life, how one interprets what one experiences, will be in part determined by what one brings to the experience in one's mind. A very real contribution to the growth of realism in the individual can be made therefore by academic study; perhaps the greatest contribution of all can be made by literature and the study of history, for the concern of both is precisely the realistic portrayal of life including reference to what is not immediately visible or quantifiable. Montague suggests that when it comes to learning how to be happy 'novels and real life [must be] our tutors' in guiding us to an awareness of the many individual paths there may be (4.5); by giving us a greater understanding and more realistic appreciation of the subtleties of people, human relationships and the workings of life in general, novels may also enable us to be happier. Needless to say advertising in all its shapes and forms is antithetical to happiness, since it deliberately distorts reality (even if only by crudely oversimplifying) and increases expectations to unrealistic levels. But advertising should not be confused with escapist elements in novels, films, television and so forth. As a matter of contingent fact, fantasy and escapism in such areas may reach a pitch at which they distort people's sense of reality, but it is quite possible to have fantasy that is recognised and enjoyed as such. The fantasy promulgated by the great era of Hollywood filmmaking was never dangerous: it provided enjoyment and nobody took it for a picture of reality. The danger lies not in fantasy as such, but in taking fantasy seriously. (It is possible that certain more formal strategies, such as the use of Strong's Unself programme (1.4, 6.5), might help to promote a more realistic awareness of other people, but there seems no reason to think them of particular importance. Realism is best developed by a realistic and honest environment.)

I should make it clear that I use the ambiguous phrase 'essential conditions' deliberately since the logic of the above elements is slightly different. A lack of self-esteem is in itself, as we have seen, logically incompatible with happiness (6.5). That is not strictly speaking true of a lack of realism and a lack of security, unless these are depicted exclusively in terms of the sort of concepts that I have argued above (5.9) are logically incompatible with happiness (e.g. anxiety, depression, frustration). One could conceive of a man who was happy but insecure, if, for example, one had in mind someone who was in a precarious position, sensed that precariousness, but was so constituted as to regard that as exhilarating rather than threatening. (One might of course choose to say of such a person that by definition he doesn't really feel insecure.) Much more certainly one could conceive of someone being happy but unrealistic, for, as has been argued, happiness can actually arise out of a false estimate of a situation. What I am concerned to convey, then, by labelling these three as 'essential conditions' is that, albeit for slightly different reasons, as human beings appear to be constituted nobody in the sort of societies with which we are familiar is going to remain happy for long while being unrealistic, feeling insecure and lacking in self-esteem.

8.5 How do we set about nurturing security, self-esteem and realism? To start at the beginning: we should surely seek to satisfy most of what Aristotle classifies as natural needs (or to provide what he called real goods) (2.2). The argument of chapter 5 suggests that it is wrong to regard food, physical health and friendship as logically necessary to the very notion of happiness (5.7). However, it is surely clear that as a matter of contingent fact most human beings' happiness will be enhanced by the satisfaction of such needs and imperilled if they are not satisfied. Aristotle also argues that curiosity and thirst for knowledge are natural needs in humans; he is probably correct in thinking that thwarting or inhibiting the element of inquiry in the child will adversely affect his chances of happiness.

The evidence concerning motivators and hygeines suggests that we should be particularly concerned to see that whatever is intrinsic to the child's school life in the early years should be suited to him, since it is the motivators that provide positive satisfaction (1.6). To control the hygeines adequately – for example to avoid making school holiday arrangements that are irksome – is necessary in order to ward off active dissatisfaction. But that is not likely to be a real issue with schoolchildren at this age: they are seldom profoundly irritated by extrinsic factors. The problem is more one of making factors intrinsic to school life positively welcome. (It is reasonable to suppose that in the later years of schooling the emphasis should shift: a sixth former is very likely to be extremely dissatisfied by some extrinsic factors, and correspondingly less likely to be rendered particularly happy by the acceptability of intrinsic factors.)

The above guidelines are not very precise, they are based upon evidence and reasoning that is far from compelling, and there is no guarantee that they will prove particularly effective in all cases. What can be said with some degree of assurance is that to act otherwise or to organise things in such a way as to go against the spirit of these guidelines would be even less likely to promote happiness. In the early years, both at home and at school, we should seek to provide the child with a sense of security, physical and emotional, and to reinforce his actual interests, while ensuring that he is not troubled or threatened by any intrinsic features of the way of life we set before him. That at any rate would constitute a good foundation for the future.

It will be noted that although there is no reason to suppose and no evidence to support the view that children granted a great amount of freedom, as at Summerhill, are not as happy as children anywhere else, there is no reason to acept the contrary thesis that a free environment is necessary to happiness in the short or the long term. In so far as children are unhappy in seemingly restricted school environments, it is not the lack of freedom as such that is the cause, but must rather be something such as the manner in which the restrictions are imposed and maintained or the specific nature of some of them. Far from it being the case that freedom is a necessary condition of happiness, all the evidence and reasoning points to the conclusion that people need a determinate environment for their happiness (6.3). Children need some sort of rule structure to their lives and they need to know where they stand in respect of it. Summerhill's democratic procedures may provide that necessity as well as any other system of school organisation as a matter of contingent fact, but they are not logically necessary to happiness. The priorities, in the case of the young child, must be to develop trust in his primary groupings, to provide security through warmth and affection and to impart understanding of the rules that govern his life.

8.6 Most of the above will continue to be of importance throughout later years of schooling too. But now comes the more interesting task of trying to take steps in the present with a view to future happiness. In looking to the future it is useful to recall Von Wright's three-fold classification of factors affecting experience of happiness: chance factors, dispositional factors and factors of human agency (4.6).

There is obviously nothing that we can do about chance factors as such. What we can do is play a part in developing dispositional traits and talents that will affect how the individual deals with whatever chances do occur and, indeed, to some extent limit the range of what can chance to occur.

To take the latter point first: we cannot prevent people chancing to die, having accidents, losing their jobs and so forth. But we can explain to people the wisdom of doing or refraining from doing some things rather than others. We can, for example, teach people not that they cannot find happiness in drink or drugs (5.7, 6.9) (which is not necessarily true), but that such sources of happiness are risky in various specifiable ways: one may become more or less dependent on them (and then perhaps unable to afford that dependency, or left at the mercy of some other agent); the source may become less effective as a source of happiness; finding happiness in this way may actively diminish one's ability to find happiness in other ways, and may finally lead one to death or sorrows in respect of other potential sources of happiness such as one's emotional life or career. In so far as we succeed in keeping people this side of addiction, though we do not necessarily make them happier in the here and now, we probably ward off a miserable end and certainly put them, in one area at least, less at the mercy of chance.

More generally, by getting people to think about the nature of happiness we can bring them to see the importance of certain strategies that are well within their grasp. For example, it is foolish to spend one's life comparing one's own lot with that of other people apparently more fortunately placed; for, inasmuch as happiness is increased and diminished not by simple changes in circumstance but by the fit or lack of it between circumstance and expectation, it is evidently folly to dwell upon circumstances that do not exist for oneself and to envisage the day that they will. It is important too, since we live in a world that changes rapidly, to bring people up to expect change and to be unconcerned by it as such.

Knowledge and understanding of various sorts, then, though they do not themselves provide or constitute happiness, may give one a greater control over some of the chance elements that do affect one's happiness.

The most important task remains that of developing certain dispositions and certain intellectual traits that have a direct bearing on one's happiness or lack of it. The dispositions most obviously required are those of determination, resignation, modesty, open-mindedness and empathy. The need for self-esteem notwithstanding, modesty is desirable inasmuch as unwarranted conceit is one of the many types of fantasy to which we may be prey; another is dogmatism, the obverse of open-mindedness. The point here is that false and inaccurate perceptions of one's own powers and one's own qualities will finally come into conflict with reality: at that point the gulf between expectation and actuality lies open. Likewise, although it is logically conceivable that dogmatic people should be happy, dogmatism is contingently at risk, if the reality consists in an open society wherein it is recognised that little can be regarded as unequivocal and certain. (Two points are perhaps worth repeating: dogmatism might actually contribute to happiness in some societies, such as closed totalitarian ones; my point relates to the reality of an open democratic society.[6] Secondly, dogmatism should not be confused with faith or commitment. The latter has been shown to be one possible source of happiness (6.5), but to believe in something is not the same thing as believing that one's belief is obviously true as all but fools can see. The latter is dogmatism.) Determination, resignation and empathy are likewise attitudes of mind or dispositional factors that affect the sum of human happiness essentially through their links with realism. To act and react realistically it is necessary to have some feeling for other people and their feelings as they actually are, which is what is meant by empathy. It is also necessary to recognise the need to have the drive to make things happen rather than passively react to things happening, while nonetheless retaining something of the stoic endurance (4.1) in the face of what is the case, has happened or must be, since such things cannot be wished away. One is indulging in fantasy and both denying and losing control of reality if one fails in the former respect (lacks determination); one is romantically unrealistic and ill-prepared for enmeshment with the circumstances of life if one is lacking in the latter respect (lacking resignation).[7]

A slightly different kind of dispositional factor that may affect one's happiness is that of interest or enthusiasm. What I mean by the disposition of interest is the tendency to look for what may be of interest in anything, rather than the cultivation of particular interests. Clearly particular interests may be sources of happiness to people, but since it is difficult to predict what will go on interesting people in the future, a much more useful thing for schools to cultivate is this characteristic of exploring the potentialities of anything one may happen to encounter. Of course, things that are in themselves a greater potential source of interest than others, perhaps because of their complexity and extent, are both better material in respect of which to cultivate the disposition and more valuable as potential long-term sources of happiness. But here, as always, there must be a correlation between individual aptitude and the demands of the activity in question: bridge will provide more interest than snap for a longer period, to a relatively sophisticated mind. To a less sophisticated mind, snap may be quite as good a source of interest. Mill's observation that there are certain relatively complex pleasures that all judges who have experience of them would place above the simpler pleasures, has this much truth in it: people who are capable of enjoying both Shakespeare and Agatha Christie are likely to regard the former as superior inasmuch as the complexity of mind necessary for appreciating it is likely to grow more quickly bored with the simple pleasure of the latter (6.2). (This is *not* to say that the latter may not give as much pleasure at a particular time.)

8.7 The intellectual traits that need to be developed are more or less those specified by Russell: understanding, rationality and an orderly mind (3.8). Misapprehension, whether of fact about the world or of beliefs, feelings and attitudes of other people, diminishes one's control over chance factors affecting happiness and gives one less chance of contributing to the happiness of others. Russell is surely correct to point out that a great deal of unhappiness is the result of unnecessary and pointless worrying, which, in turn, may be the product of a badly ordered mind that is in itself unrealistic. But the term rationality, if interpreted broadly, is by far the most important. This is rationality not simply in the sense of the ability to reason, but with the important addition of the *will* to reason and the ability to do it *well.* And rationality in this sense should be seen not as something opposed to emotion but as something that organises, orders and controls emotion. The picture here is very Platonic:[8] happiness depends upon realistic appraisals of situations, realistic predictions and the realistic ordering of desires, and rationality is necessary to each of those objectives. Support for the rational element is to be found in the determination and resignation that are aspects of the will. To be sure of your own happiness you need to have the strength of purpose to follow a realistic ordering of your desires; to contribute to that of others you need to endure in the task of seeking to do so in a realistic manner.

It is these intellectual traits that are the crucial human agency factors relating to happiness.

8.8 It remains only to comment on ways in which one might increase the chances of providing present happiness and nurturing the qualities referred to. Russell remarks that most people need sympathetic surroundings for their happiness (3.7).[9] That they must perceive their surroundings to be sympathetic can now be seen to be tautologous: to be happy is (understood in the way and with the qualifications explained in chapter 5) more or less to see one's circumstances as sympathetic. But if Russell means that happiness would generally be increased by an environment providing kindness and encouragement in objective terms, then his claim, no longer tautologous, may have something in it. If we take the evidence of Young and Jokiel into account (1.6), we may add that ideally the physical environment of the school should be pleasant too: Papadatos, it is true, provides no evidence to support his specific contention about the need for coordinated bright colour schemes (1.4), and to some of us it may seem rather unlikely that the drab classrooms of Victorian schools were themselves a cause of relative unhappiness; nonetheless, on balance, it seems that there is a case, in terms of happiness, for bright and cheerful buildings and staff.

Psychologists may not misrepresent the situation with their claims that authoritarianism is antithetical to happiness, but in so far as this is demonstrated to be the case it can only be a contingent fact about our society as it is now (1.6). The explanation must lie in the fact that we are brought up to be familiar with and to expect freedom, and we therefore resent the heavy hand of authoritarianism. The evidence clearly shows that this is not inevitable and that states and classrooms that lack freedom may nonetheless provide happiness (1.4, 6.3). Therefore, without necessarily advocating schooling on the Russian model, we must deny the suggestion that it is necessary to remove the (alleged) current 'Collectivist totalitarian tendency of education to gain happiness'.[10] Schools need to develop self-esteem and self-confidence in children but such objectives do not demand such techniques as self-determination, discovery learning or any great degree of freedom. (They do not preclude such techniques either.) The truth is that in terms of happiness alone the provision of a great or a minimal amount of freedom is neither here nor there. What matters in the present is that children should know the limits of their freedom, whatever they may be. What matters for the future is that by the end of their schooling students should have become used to exercising the degree of self-discipline and the degree of responsibility that society expects of and allows to its citizens generally.

Russell had slight difficulty deciding where to stand in relation to the usual competitive ethos of schools. A part of him always believed that man needs a challenge to be truly happy and that therefore competition was a healthy aspect of communal life; another part of him was dismayed by the competitive structure of schools (3.7). There is no doubt, however, where the truth lies: the competitive element institutionalised in school life (and our society generally) must be a hindrance to happiness overall. This is not to deny that some people may gain their happiness through competition and others in spite of it, or that it may be useful as a means to other ends, some of which might even in their turn serve happiness. But happiness cannot be enhanced by competition in itself, because a competitive setting by its nature teaches us to look at our own life in comparative terms, encourages the majority of us to feel inadequate as failures and invites us to feel envious. Competition in schools is the educational equivalent of advertising. One may reasonably set targets and make judgements, so the notion of standards and assessment is not necessarily rejected here, but in the interests of happiness a competitive setting should be rejected in schools.

Obviously it helps, superficially at least, to diminish students' anxieties about known sources of worry, such as their work and, at later stages, their financial circumstances and various personal relationships. There is no point in *not* trying to alleviate such tensions. However it is important to recognise that allaying specific worries is one of the least effective general strategies for the maximising of happiness. To enable people to become happier people you need to teach them to stop worrying, rather than to remove their immediate worries. A worry (anxiety, concern, etc.) is not simply an objective phenomenon such as a pregnant girlfriend or a forgotten piece of homework; it involves a particular attitude to that objective phenomenon. The person who is worried by the fact that his girlfriend is pregnant would worry about something else if she were not. We do not therefore make a real contribution to the long-term happiness of students (of whatever age) by relieving them of or cushioning them from specific anxieties.

The notion that one might increase happiness, one's own or other people's, by engaging in a simulation game based on the concept of happiness, seems absurd (1.4). The weakness in the idea is the same that is to be found in the idea of deliberately searching for happiness. The truth behind the adage that happiness is the reward of those who are not looking for it is surely that happiness does not consist in the recognition that one is happy, but in the very often unselfconscious sense of enmeshment. To search for happiness betrays a misunderstanding of what it is. It is not something that can be looked for: it is the outcome of you and the world being in a harmonious relationship with one another. Therefore what we have to learn are ways of being in harmony with the world rather than ways of grasping happiness. What we should be doing is taking one idea from Aristotle in cultivating certain virtuous habits and another from Plato in developing the rational element in the individual, for in the end it is surprising how much the continued happiness of us all (that most emotional and romantic seeming aim) is dependent upon reliable patterns of behaviour and intellect.

Certain ways of behaving are generally antithetical to happiness in a society such as ours. Various forms of physical aggression are a case in point. In so far as we are convinced by the evidence that exercise, such as that involved in organised games, channels out aggression and that aggressive tendencies can be trained out (as well as aggressive actions) by a process of restraining the actions (1.6), we have a case for saying that schools should encourage games and actively prevent other unorganised forms of aggressive behaviour.[11] Equally, children should be encouraged to perform acts that bring happiness to others, so that the performance of such acts becomes habitual. Other character traits too, such as what we may unflatteringly refer to as maintenance of the stiff upper lip, should be developed. For, in so far as the individual who has been trained to display the stiff upper lip also has more real control of his reactions, his control over his happiness is greater. People who are realistic enough to expect setbacks in life and who are used to controlling their dismayed reaction to such setbacks are less vulnerable to unhappiness than those who react to every upset like a baby denied its feed.

It is important to note that despite widespread opinion to the contrary, and despite the caution deployed earlier in this book about the connection between education and happiness, there is evidence that education, conceived of in terms of the promotion of knowledge and understanding for their own sakes, can make a direct contribution to personal happiness. For we have evidence that low cognitive, inflexible and extremist people are relatively unhappy (1.7). (That is anyway what we would expect since such characteristics involve one being relatively lacking in realism and relatively ill-suited to an open society.) Education is more or less precisely designed to remove such characteristics. Such people of course are also unlikely to contribute much to the happiness of others.

Although there is not a great deal more that can be said about it, the importance of the intellectual development of people in respect of happiness cannot be overemphasised. We have to give people knowledge and awareness of other people and of how different from our own their assumptions and attitudes may be; we have to give people understanding of themselves; we have to impart information about the world such that the likely consequences of actions can be realistically assessed; and we have to develop in people the ability to think rationally. Those intellectual qualities guarantee nothing and are certainly not necessary conditions of happiness. But in an open society they are contingently very likely to increase happiness overall, for they give us collectively and individually the opportunity to control our future happiness.

The empirical evidence does not settle the question of whether, in school or anywhere else, people work well because they are happy or rather are happy because their work is successful (1.6). Commonsense and personal experience, however, would suggest that the evidence is inconclusive because the matter cannot be seen as one of two incompatible alternatives, but must rather be seen as one of spiralling interplay. Happy children are likely to work better and successful work is likely to prove a source of happiness. The very clear evidence that people are happier when they have work to do that is suited to their capabilities than when they do not (1.6) though it cannot be used crudely as an argument for streaming in schools (even were happiness our paramount concern), does involve the corollary that any teaching or learning arrangement that involves some children being either over- or under-stretched is detrimental to the immediate happiness of those particular children.

Finally there is the question of the use of drugs and other similarly physical means of inducing happiness in schools. I have argued above (6.9) that some at least of such means must be admitted to lead to or contribute to happiness, and in certain circumstances it would seem to me quite legitimate, even desirable, to make use of them. However, there can be no case for using them in a specifically educational context, for though a drug may bring happiness it is inherently antithetical to any truly educational process, the latter being, by definition, intimately involved with understanding and reason, while the former by its nature subdues and diminishes the rational element in us.

8.9 My conclusion, unarresting but, I hope compelling, amounts to this: happiness is not logically tied to any particular conditions, and should not be thought of in terms of a particular feeling. It is nothing more and nothing less than a sense of enmeshment with one's circumstances. It is something to be valued and schools should show concern for it, particularly for long-term happiness. To provide people with a secure environment, nurture their self-esteem and give them a realistic outlook on life is both to contribute to their happiness and to give them something of the wherewithal to maintain it. Those objectives may be achieved by an upbringing that takes the emphasis off competitive achievement in respect of a limited range of values and replaces it with an emphasis on encouraging self-esteem and cooperation. But in the long run a most important consideration is the development in children of the particular dispositions and intellectual qualities referred to. Happiness does not logically depend upon them exclusively, but as a matter of fact our long-term happiness in an open society probably does depend upon them.

I have assumed throughout the course of the second half of this book that the alleged biological foundations of irrationality are not insurmountable in so far as they exist (1.4), at any rate to the extent that there are active steps that we can take that may materially affect the degree of rationality that people come to display in their lives. I have also conducted the inquiry within the context of an open society such as that of Britain, because, presumably, many people will be primarily interested in increasing happiness without radically altering the nature of society. But I cannot permit myself to finish this book without emphasising that it is a superficial judgement that thinks that the open society is necessarily more conducive to individual happiness, as defined, than the closed society. Logically, as I have argued elsewhere,[12] the completely happy society could well be totalitarian in nature and might even owe its happiness to its totalitarian nature. Empirically, relatively closed societies and communities have been shown to be as happy or happier than relatively open ones (1.4). Following on from those observations, I would argue that in so far as happiness is really a matter of concern to us there are more significant steps that might be taken than those referred to in the context of schooling. The best way to increase our happiness would be either to regenerate faith in our capitalistic, competitive and unequal society (amongst all people, including the losers) or to change the circumstances. It is hard to think of a better recipe for unhappiness than what some would see as the present situation: a community that is geared to increasing our expectations and our desire for limited goods, and that is increasingly failing both to meet the raised expectations and to generate commitment to the system itself (as opposed to the hoped-for rewards). I would hazard the opinion that the day has (thankfully) gone when one could seriously expect the majority so to believe in the competitive system that they really did not see themselves as hard done by, and really did not feel envious of the more fortunate or anxious at their own poverty. That being so the only realistic option is to clamp down on the competitive system, the advertising attitude and the patent inequalities in material wealth to be found in this society.

In the meantime, if we restrict ourselves to what improvements we can bring about through schooling, we must remember the importance of regenerating faith in schooling and education themselves. Russell acutely appreciated that the scientific community (at the date he was writing) gained a great deal of happiness from the fact that they did work and participated in a way of life that were widely taken to be important: that fact alone gave them an all-important injection of self-esteem (3.8). There is a case for saying that teachers are currently rather lacking in self-esteem, partly because they are in fact not held in such esteem by the community as a whole as they have sometimes been, partly because they sense they are one of the sections of society with relatively little industrial muscle, and partly because there are many real problems, doubts and difficulties to be resolved in their line of business. Such (relative) lack of confidence and consequent diminution of satisfaction is very likely to communicate itself to children and schooling as a whole. Certainly those professionally involved with education today resemble the artist more than the scientist of Russell's example. There are few people who don't have their own answers to the problems of schooling and education — few people, that is to say, who would not tend to see the teacher with whom they disagree as they see the artist with whom they disagree (inept rather than more knowledgeable), rather than as they see the scientist (more knowledgeable). It seems to me undeniable that the immediate happiness of all concerned and the strength of the foundations for making a further contribution to happiness will be increased in proportion to the degree to which the whole enterprise of education can find faith in itself again.

Finally, there is one other thing we might profitably teach about, and that is the nature of happiness itself. Too many people miss out on happiness because they assume that it is something it is not or because they have some other, false, ideas about it: they await some unique magical feeling, perhaps, and their fretting about the absence of that stands in the way of their being enmeshed; they believe that it must come through wealth or virtue, maybe, and simply find themselves mistaken; they are convinced that it doesn't count if happiness is based on simple pleasures, so they avoid some of the things that would actually make them happy. These, and a hundred other erroneous beliefs about happiness, themselves stop people being happy. And such beliefs could be removed by thinking about the concept of happiness. For, when all is said and done, as it now has been, it is a material comfort in itself to know and understand wise words such as these of Erasmus: 'It is the chiefest point of happiness that a man is willing to be what he is.'

Notes and References

PART I: Background Material

1 Empirical Claims

1 Stephen K. Bailey 'Educational purpose and the pursuit of happiness' *Phi Delta Kappan* (September 1976)
2 Broadus N. Butler 'The pursuit of happiness not pleasure' *Crisis* (May 1976)
3 'Educating our children for life, liberty and the pursuit of happiness' *Journal of Teacher Education* (Winter 1976)
4 Sam J. Ervin, Jr 'The pursuit of happiness' *NASSP Bulletin* (May 1977)
5 P. Ashton *et al. The Aims of Primary Education: A Study of Teachers' Opinions* (London: Macmillan, 1975)
6 Arline Sakuma McCord 'Happiness as educational equality' *Society* (November - December 1974)
7 H.C. Kramer, F. Berger, G. Miller 'Student concerns and sources of assistance' *Journal of College Student Personnel* (September 1974)
8 Quoted in A.V. Judges (ed.) *Pioneers of English Education* (London: Faber, 1952) p. 93
9 Quoted in W.H. Burton (ed.) *James Hill on Education* (Cambridge: Cambridge University Press, 1969) p. 41
10 Lewis Rutherford 'Notes on educational theory' *Journal of West Virginia Philosophy Society* (Fall 1974)
11 See Plato *Republic* (trans. Desmond Lee, Harmondsworth: Penguin, 1974); Rousseau *Emile* (trans. Barbara Foxley, London: Dent, 1972)
12 Bailey 'Educational purpose and the pursuit of happiness' *op. cit.*
13 A.S. Neill *Summerhill* (Harmondsworth: Penguin, 1968)
14 S.P. Papadatos 'Color them motivated - color's psychological effects on students' *NASSP Bulletin* (February 1973)
15 Gordon A. MacLeod 'Does creativity lead to happiness and more enjoyment of life?' *The Journal of Creative Behavior* (4th Quarter, 1973)
16 See Kramer, Berger, Miller 'Student concerns and sources of assistance' *op. cit.*
17 D. Blazer, E. Palmore 'Religion and aging in a longitudinal panel' *Gerontologist* (February 1976)
18 Wayne O. Evans 'Mind-altering drugs and the future' *The Futurist* (June 1971)
19 Bailey 'Educational purpose and the pursuit of happiness' *op. cit.*

20 Butler 'The pursuit of happiness not pleasure' *op. cit.*
21 Ralph P. Davidson 'Education in a changing economy' *Education Tomorrow* no. 6 (New York: College Entrance Examination Board, 1975)
22 Keith Goldhammer 'Curriculum imperatives for meaningful education' *OSSC Bulletin* 20, No. 8 (April 1977)
23 Albert Ellis 'The biological basis of human irrationality' paper presented at the Annual Meeting of the American Psychological Association (August 1975)
24 Hans A. Schieser 'De-socialising school instead of deschooling society' paper presented at the National Convention of the American Educational Studies Association (November 1975)
25 Francis L.K. Hsu *Americans and Chinese: Reflections on Two Cultures and their People* (New York: Doubleday Natural History Press, 1972)
26 Philip H. Gillespie *Learning Through Simulation Games* (New Jersey: Paulist Press, 1973)
27 William Strong 'Unself' *Media and Methods* (November 1974)
28 D. Wessmann 'A psychological inquiry into satisfaction and happiness' unpublished doctoral dissertation (Princeton University, 1956); cf. H. Cantril *The Pattern of Human Concerns* (New Brunswick: Rutgers University Press, 1965)
29 Craig Mosher 'Woodworker' *Humanist* (January - February 1975)
30 Bailey 'Educational purpose and the pursuit of happiness' *op. cit.*
31 Kramer, Berger, Miller 'Student concerns and sources of assistance' *op. cit.*
32 B. Balinsky and J.H. Finkelman in B.B. Wolman (ed.) *Handbook of General Psychology* (New Jersey: Prentice-Hall, 1973)
33 R.G. Landry and E.M. Pardew 'Self concept enhancement of preschool children' paper presented at the Annual Meeting of the American Educational Research Association (New Orleans, February 1973)
34 B.J. Jokiel and John Starkey 'Effect of a school-within-a-school program on attitudes of underachieving students' *EDRS* (1972)
35 See Wolman (ed.) *Handbook of General Psychology op. cit.*, esp. pp. 937-9
36 Cited by Balinsky and Finkelman in Wolman (ed.)
37 Ibid. p. 938
38 P.T. Young in Wolman (ed.), p. 756
39 W. Wilson quoted by Young in Wolman (ed.)
40 J.P. Scott in Wolman (ed.) p. 716
41 G. Lenski and J. Leggett 'Caste, class and deference in the research interview' *American Journal of Sociology* (1960). Referred to in John P. Robinson and Phillip R. Shaver *Measures of Social Psychological Attitudes* (Ann Arbor Michigan: Institute for Social Research, 1978). This volume incorporates most, if not all, of the attitudinal studies of happiness and related concepts.
42 D. Wessman 'A psychological inquiry into satisfaction and happiness' *op. cit.*
43 Quoted by Nicholas Rescher 'The environmental crisis and the quality of life' in W.T. Blackstone (ed.) *Philosophy and the Environmental Crisis* (Athens: University of Georgia, 1974)
44 *Ibid.*
45 All the information in the above two paragraphs and the reports of the research behind it are to be found in Robinson and Shaver *Measures of social psychological attitudes op. cit.*

2 Aristotle on Happiness

1 Aristotle *Nichomachean Ethics,* (transl. J.A.K. Thomson, Harmondsworth: Penguin Books, 1976)

2 References are made according to the traditional paginal markings of the Greek text. These references are retained in the Penguin translation.

3 Aristotle *Nichomachean Ethics op. cit.* 1094 a 18

4 G.E.M. Anscombe *Intention* (London: Oxford University Press, 1957) *ff* 21. cf. P.T. Geach *Journal of the Philosophical Association* 5 (1958) p. 112. For a rather different view see Anthony Kenny 'Aristotle on happiness' in Jonathan Barnes, Malcolm Schofield, Richard Sorabji (eds) *Articles on Aristotle* vol. 2. (London: Duckworth, 1977)

5 H.A. Prichard, *Moral Obligation* (London: Oxford University Press, 1968) pp. 51-2 (originally appeared in *Philosophy* 1935). In the original, Prichard uses the Greek words when referring to Aristotle.

6 W.F.R. Hardie *Aristotle's Ethical Theory* (London: Oxford University Press, 1968) p. 22

7 Aristotle *Posterior Analytics II,* 8 and 9

8 J.A. Broyer 'Aristotle: is happiness ambiguous?' *Midwestern Journal of Philosophy* (Spring 1973)

9 Herodotus *The Histories* (trans. Aubrey de Selincourt, Harmondsworth: Penguin, 1954) 1.32

10 R.C. Solomon 'Is there happiness after death?' *Philosophy* 51 (April 1976)

3 Some Literary Aphorisms

1 Eric Partridge *A Dictionary of Clichés* (London: Routledge and Kegan Paul, 1978) p. 2. Examples of the sort of 'quoteable quotes' book I have in mind include: Frank Muir *The Frank Muir Book* (London: Heinemann, 1976), Valerie Ferguson *Sayings of the week* (London: David and Charles, 1978); Nigel Rees *'Quote . . . Unquote'* (London: Allen and Unwin, 1978); Kenneth Edwards *I wish I'd said that* (London: Abelard, 1976); Nancy McPhee *The Book of Insults* (New York and London: Paddington Press, 1978).

2 R.F. Dearden 'Happiness and education' *The Philosophy of Education Society of Great Britain: Proceedings of the Annual Conference* (1967)

3 R.F. Dearden 'On happiness: reply to R. Barrow' unpublished paper delivered at Annual Conference of the Philosophy of Education Society of Great Britain (1976)

4 Theodore Benditt 'Happiness' *Philosophical Studies* 25 (January 1974)

5 Garth Hallett 'Happiness' *The Heythrop Journal* (July 1971)

6 Agatha Christie *Sparkling Cyanide* Collected edition (London: Hamlyn, 1970) p. 70; cf. her explicit discussion of the theme of happiness in *The Burden,* one of her romantic novels written under the name Mary Westmacott.

7 Nicholas Rescher 'The environmental crisis and the quality of life' in W.T. Blackstone (ed.) *Philosophy and the Environmental Crisis* (Athens: University of Georgia, 1974); Samuel Butler *The Way of All Flesh* (New York: Signet, 1960)

8 J.H. Randall 'The "really" real' *The Journal of Philosophy, Psychology and Scientific Methods* (June 1920)

9 J.L. Austin *Sense and Sensibilia* (London: Oxford University Press, 1962); Keith Graham *J.L. Austin* (Sussex: Harvester Press, 1978); Ernest Gellner

Words and things (London: Gollancz, 1959); J. Bennett 'Real' *Mind* No. 75 (1966); see below Irwin Goldstein, ch. 5.7.

10 Archytas (fl. 400 BC) Stobaeus *Florilegium* 1.70
11 Seneca (BC 1 - AD 65) *De vita beata* XVI.1; Cicero (BC 106 - 43) *De natura deorum* 1.18.48
12 *De vita beata* V.2.
13 Archytas, Stobaeus *Florileguim* 1.79; Cicero *Epistola ad Corneluim Nepotem* (Fragment IV)
14 Seneca *Ad Lucilium epistulae morales* XCII
15 Theognis (BC 570-490) *Sententiae* 167; Sophocles (BC 495-406) Fragment 572, *Trachineae* 1, *Oedipus* 1528; Euripides (BC 481-406) *Andromache* 100, *Troades* 509
16 Euripides *Peleus* Fragment
17 Ovid (BC 43 - AD 18) *Metamorphoses* III. 135
18 Seneca *Ad Lucilium epistulae morales* XCII. 3
19 Juvenal (fl. c.90 AD) *Satires* XIII. 20
20 Henry Vaughan (1622-1695): 'Happy in those early days, when I Shin'd in my angel infancy.' (*Silex Scintillans,* The Retreat, 1)
21 Thomas Gray (1716-1771) *Ode on a distant prospect of Eton College* 1.92
22 William Shakespeare (1546-1616) *King Henry VI* pt. III, 11. v.21
23 Horace (BC 65-8) *Epodes* 11.1
24 Shakespeare *Othello* 111.111.346
25 Bernard Shaw (1856-1950) *Arms and the Man* Act 3
26 Erasmus (1467-1536); quoted by Rudolph Flesch (ed.) *The Book of Unusual Quotations* (London: Cassell, 1959)
27 Aldous Huxley *Point Counter Point* ch. 30
28 William Feather, quoted by Rudolph Flesch *op. cit.*
29 Luc Marquis de Vauvenargues (1715-1747) *ibid.*
30 Charles Louis de Montesquieu (1689-1755) *ibid.* cf. 'Suppose a man were eating rotten stockfish, the very smell of which would choke another, and yet believed it a dish for the gods, what difference is there as to his happiness?'
31 Edward de Bono, quoted in the *Observer* 12 June 1977
32 William Wordsworth (1770-1850) *Character of the Happy Warrior*
33 Henry Wotton (1568-1639) *Character of a Happy Life* VI
34 Thomas Dekker (1570-1641) *Patient Grissil* Act 1
35 John Dryden (1631-1700) *The Indian Emperor* IV.1
36 Samuel Johnson (1709-1784); quoted in Flesch, *op. cit.*
37 Leo Tolstoy (1828-1910) *ibid.*
38 Bernard Shaw (1856-1950) *Man and Superman,* Act 1
39 Alexander Pope (1688-1744) *An Essay on Man* Ep IV.1
40 Francis Hutcheson (1694-1746) *Inquiry into the Origin of our Ideas of Beauty and Virtue* Treatise II, see 3.8
41 Richard Owen Cambridge (1717-1802) *Learning l.* 23
42 Alfred Tennyson (1809-1892) *The Coming of Arthur*
43 John Milton (1608-1674) *Paradise Lost* 8.364
44 Ben Jonson (1573-1637) *Cynthia's Revels* III.2
45 Samuel Butler (1835-1902) Quoted in Flesch, *op. cit.*
46 Bertrand Russell *The Conquest of Happiness* (London: Allen and Unwin, 1975)
47 Bertrand Russell 'Philosophy and politics' in *Unpopular Essays* (London: Allen and Unwin, 1950)
48 Attention should be drawn to a recent book similar in type to Russell's

Conquest of Happiness: Paul Kurtz's *Exuberance: A Philosophy of Happiness* (New York: Prometheus Books, 1977). The main thing to stress is that 'Exhuberance' is the right word, for despite the sub-title 'a philosophy of happiness' this book is really concerned with exuberance, which, as I shall argue in chapter 5, is merely one species or form of happiness. Like Russell, Kurtz is concerned with tips for achieving exuberance rather than with any serious philosophical inquiry into the matter. He says much that Russell says, but is even more populist and superficial (without necessarily being mistaken). Thus we are treated to a chapter on Eroticism, which seems largely designed merely to reassure people who may have minority sexual interests by listing such interests and indicating that the author for one does not classify them as perverted. Such sentiments and indeed such reassurance are in my view admirable, but such an approach does not make for a very interesting book. I hope that I am correct in thinking that it is the nature of the book (its style, its aims, its presentation) that leads me to dismiss it as unimportant in this context, rather than its viewpoint. But it must be admitted that it does embody a viewpoint (to the effect that creative achievement, activity and freedom are necessary to happiness) that I do not share. I might concede that such features are necessary to exuberance, but not to happiness unless that is taken to be synonymous with exuberance. (See below chapters 4 and 5.) Cf J. Freedman *Happy People: What Happiness Is, Who Has It and Why* (New York: Harcourt, Brace, 1979)

4 The Philosophical Tradition

1 Discourses of Epictetus Book IV, ch. IV. For a complete collection of the extant sources for stoicism and epicureanism see Whitney J. Oates (ed.) *The Stoic and Epicurean Philosophers* (New York: Random House, 1940)
2 Boethius *The Consolation of Philosophy* (transl. V.E. Watts, Harmondsworth: Penguin, 1969)
3 Thomas Hobbes (1588-1679) *Human Nature.* See R.S. Peters (ed.) *Body, Man and Citizen* (New York: Collier Macmillan, 1962) p. 209
4 John Locke (1632-1704) *An Essay Concerning Human Nature* 2.21.41 (ed. A. Woozley, London: Fontana, 1964, p. 173)
5 Jeremy Bentham (1748-1832) *Principles of Morals and Legislation* ch. 1 (New York: Hafner, 1965)
6 John Stuart Mill (1806-1873) *Utilitarianism* ch. 2 (ed. M. Warnock, London: Fontana, 1962, p. 257)
7 *Ibid.*
8 J.F. Narveson, *Morality and Utility* Baltimore: John Hopkins University Press, 1967)
9 A. MacIntyre 'Against utilitarianism' in T. Hollins (ed.) *Aims in Education* (Manchester University Press, 1964). See my critical comments on MacIntyre in R. Barrow *Common Sense and the Curriculum* (London: Allen and Unwin, 1976) ch. 3
10 G.H. Von Wright *The Varieties of Goodness* (London: Routledge and Kegan Paul, 1963)
11 Jean Austin 'Pleasure and happiness' *Philosophy* 43 (January 1968)
12 Anthony Kenny 'Happiness' *Proceedings of the Aristotelian Society* 66 (1965-6)
13 R.M. Hare *Freedom and Reason* (London: Oxford University Press, 1965) p. 128

14 Roger Montague 'Happiness' *Proceedings of the Aristotelian Society* 67 (1966-7)
15 John Wilson 'Happiness' *Analysis* 29 (1968) p. 16
16 D.A. Lloyd Thomas 'Happiness' *The Philosophical Quarterly* 18, no. 71 (April 1968)
17 R.F. Dearden 'Happiness and education' *The Philosophy of Education Society of Great Britain: Proceedings of the Annual Conference* (1967)
18 Theodore Benditt 'Happiness' *Philosophical Studies* 25 (January 1974)
19 Robert W. Simpson 'Happines' *American Philosophical Quarterly* (April 1975)
20 Irwin Goldstein 'Happiness: the role of non-hedonic criteria in its evaluation' *International Philosophical Quarterly* 13 (1973)

PART II: Some Positive Conclusions

5 The Concept Analysed

1 John Wilson 'Happiness' *Analysis* 29 (1968) p. 13
2 D.A. Lloyd Thomas 'Happiness' *Philosophical Quarterly* 18, no. 71 (April 1968)
3 R.F. Dearden 'Happiness and education' *The Philosophy of Education Society of Great Britain: Proceedings of the Annual Conference* (1967)
4 Lloyd Thomas 'Happiness' *op. cit.*
5 Alexander Pope *An Essay on Man* Ep. IV.1
6 Theodore Benditt 'Happiness' *Philosophical Studies* 25 (January 1974)
7 Lewis Carroll 'The Hunting of the Snark':
In the midst of the word he was trying to say
In the midst of his laughter and glee
He had softly and suddenly vanished away -
For the Snark *was* a Boojum, you see.
8 R. Montague 'Happiness' *Proceedings of the Aristotelian Society* 67; (1966-67); Robert W. Simpson 'Happiness' *American Philosophical Quarterly* (April 1975)
9 Wilson 'Happiness' *op. cit.*
10 Brian Barry *Political Argument* (London: Routledge and Kegan Paul, 1965) p. 41: 'Someone may be satisfying a large number of wants but still not be accounted happy if the pattern arising from satisfying these wants adds up to what is thought of as a radically vicious style of life.'
11 J. Austin 'Pleasure and happiness' *Philosophy* 43 (January 1968); R.M. Hare *Freedom and Reason* (London: Oxford University Press, 1965); Simpson 'Happiness' *op. cit.;* Irwin Goldstein 'Happiness: the role of non-hedonic criteria in its evaluation' *International Philosophical Quarterly* 13 (1973)
12 Bertrand Russell *The Conquest of Happiness* (London: Allen & Unwin, 1975)
13 G.H. Von Wright *Varieties of Goodness* (London: Routledge & Kegan Paul, 1963) p. 98
14 J.J. Rousseau *Emile* (trans. Barbara Foxley, London: Dent, 1972) p. 44
15 Benditt 'Happiness' *op. cit.* p. 19
16 Von Wright *Varieties of Goodness op. cit.* p. 93
17 J.P. Robinson and P.R. Shaver *Measures of Social Psychological Attitudes* (Ann Arbor, Michigan: Institute for Social Research, 1978) p. 30
18 Dearden 'Happiness and education' *op. cit.* p. 19

19 Goldstein 'Happiness: the role of non-hedonic criteria in its evaluation' *op. cit.*
20 *Ibid.*, p. 525
21 Lloyd Thomas 'Happiness' *op. cit.*
22 *Ibid.*, p. 106
23 Austin 'Pleasure and happiness' *op. cit.*; John McPeck 'Can Robin Barrow be happy and not know it?' *Proceedings of the American Philosophy of Education Society* (1978).
24 McPeck 'Can Robin Barrow be happy and not know it?' *op. cit.*
25 *Ibid.*
26 Von Wright *Varieties of Goodness op. cit.*
27 R. Barrow *Plato, Utilitarianism and Education* (London: Routledge and Kegan Paul, 1975) p. 56. This claim should not be confused with the admission (above 5.12) that what is taken to be a pattern of rejective behaviour may in fact have some other explanation.

6 *The Empirical Claims Examined*

1 Stephen K. Bailey 'Educational purpose and the pursuit of happiness' *Phi Delta Kappan* (September 1976)
2 Sam J. Ervin 'The pursuit of happiness' *NASSP Bulletin* (May 1977) p. 128
3 Hans A. Schieser 'De-socialising school instead of deschooling society' paper presented at the National Convention of the American Educational Studies Association (October/November 1975); A.S. Neill *Summerhill* (Harmondsworth: Penguin, 1968)
4 Plato *Republic* (trans. Desmond Lee, Harmondsworth: Penguin, 1974); Erich Fromm *Fear of Freedom* (London: Routledge & Kegan Paul, 1942); Urie Bronfenbrenner *Two Worlds of Childhood: USA and USSR* (London: Allen & Unwin, 1971); Francis L.K. Hsu *'Americans and Chinese: Reflections on Two Cultures and Their People* (New York: Doubleday, 1972)
5 J.S. Mill 'On Liberty' in M. Warnock (ed.) *Utilitarianism* (London: Fontana, 1962)
6 Broadus N. Butler 'The pursuit of happiness not pleasure' *Crisis* (May 1976) p. 173
7 See, e.g., S.A. Stouffer *et. al. The American Soldier* vols 1-4 (Princeton: Princeton University Press, 1949) and J.P. Robinson, P.R. Shaver *Measures of Social Psychological Attitudes* (Ann Arbor, Michigan: Institute for Social Research, 1978) p. 15
8 Butler, *op. cit.*, p. 177. The following quotations in this paragraph are from the same paper.
9 'Educating our children for life, liberty and the pursuit of happiness' *Journal of Teacher Education* (Winter, 1976) p. 299
10 *Ibid.*
11 Ralph P. Davidson 'Education in a changing economy' *Education Tomorrow* no. 6 (New York: College Entrance Examination Board, 1975)
12 B.J. Jokiel and John Starkey 'Effect of a school-within-a-school program on attitudes of underachieving students' *EDRS* (1972)
13 Anne Constantinople 'Some correlates of average level of happiness among college students' *Developmental Psychology* (May 1970)
14 H.C. Kramer, F. Berger, G. Miller 'Student concerns and sources of assistance' *Journal of College Student Personnel* (September 1974)

15 B.K. Houston 'Sources effects and individual vulnerability of psychological problems for college students' *Journal of Counseling Psychology* 18, no. 2 (1971)
16 R.G. Landry and E.M. Pardew 'Self-concept enhancement of preschool children' paper presented at the Annual Meeting of the American Educational Research Association (New Orleans, February 1973)
17 William Strong 'Unself' *Media and Methods* (November 1974)
18 Gordon A. MacLeod 'Does creativity lead to happiness and more enjoyment of life?' *Journal of Creative Behavior* (4th Quarter, 1973)
19 D. Blazer and E. Palmore 'Religion and aging in a longitudinal panel' *Gerontologist* (February 1976) p. 82
20 G. Mathiasen 'The role of religion in the lives of older people' New York State Governor's Conference on Problems of the Ageing (New York, 1955).
21 Blazer and Palmore 'Religion and aging in a longitudinal panel', *op. cit.*, p.84
22 P. Lazarsfeld 'The American Soldier – an expository review' *Public Opinion Quarterly* Vol XIII (Fall 1949)
23 Cited in *Institute for Social Research Newsletter* (University of Michigan, 2, no. 2, Summer 1974) p. 3. But cf. 6.4 above and n7.
24 'All studies indicate married people to be significantly happier than unmarried people', Robinson and Shaver point out (*Measures of Social Psychological Attitudes, op. cit.*, p. 17). However, while the Institute for Social Research report referred to in the text sees family life as a significant domain, Robinson and Shaver cite evidence that indicates an important qualification: under a half of Cantril's sample (H. Cantril, *The Pattern of Human Concerns,* New Brunswick, Rutgers University Press, 1965) mentioned family contentment and good health in describing their best possible lives, while in terms of the worst possible life poor health was mentioned far more (*Measures of Social Psychological Attitudes, op. cit.*, p. 15)
25 *Institute for Social Research Newsletter, op. cit.*, p. 5
26 *Ibid.*, p. 6
27 B.B. Wolman (ed.) *Handbook of General Psychology* (New Jersey: Prentice-Hall, 1973) p. 938. All the research cited in the above paragraphs is cited in this volume or contained in Robinson and Shaver *Measures of Social Psychological Attitudes, op. cit.*
28 W. Wilson, quoted by P.T. Young in Wolman (ed.) *Handbook of General Psychology, op. cit.*
29 Nicholas Rescher 'The environmental crisis and the quality of life' in W.T. Blackstone (ed.) *Philosophy and the Environmental Crisis* (Athens: University of Georgia, 1974)
30 Wayne O Evans 'Mind-altering drugs and the future' *The Futurist* (June 1971) p. 101
31 S. Schacter, J. Singer 'Cognitive, social and physiological determinants of emotional state' *Psychological Review* 69 (1962)
32 Evans 'Mind-altering drugs and the future' *op. cit.* p. 102.
33 G. Pitcher 'The awfulness of pain' *The Journal of Philosophy* (July 1970); Roland Puccetti 'The sensation of pleasure' *British Journal of Philosophy and Science* 20 (1969)
34 'The perception of pain' *Scientific American* (February 1961)
35 See Melzack and Wall 'Gate control theory of pain' in A. Soulairac, J. Cahn and J. Charpentier (eds.) *Pain* (New York and London: Academic Press, 1968)

36 Stephen J. Noren and Arlis Davis 'Pitcher on the awfulness of pain' *Philosophical Studies* 25 (February 1974)
37 Pucetti 'The sensation of pleasure' *op. cit.*
38 Alan E. Fuchs 'The production of pleasure by stimulation of the brain: an alleged conflict between science and philosophy' *Philosophy and Phenomenological Research* (July 1976)

7 The Value of Happiness

1 D.C. Butler 'An analysis of the values and value systems reported by students, the general public and educators in a selected Appalachian public school district' PhD dissertation, Michigan State University (1973)
2 Boris Blai, Jnr 'Two-year college faculties: their values and perceptions and values and perceptions of public and private junior college students' (Harcum Junior College, Pa.: Report No: IRR-73-14)
3 'The Mood of American Youth' report of the National Association of Secondary School Principals, Washington, DC (1974)
4 R.F. Dearden 'Happiness and education' *The Philosophy of Education Society of Great Britain: Proceedings of the Annual Conference* (1967) p.21
5 John Stuart Mill *Utilitarianism* in M. Warnock (ed.) *Utilitarianism* (London: Fontana, 1962) pp. 288ff.
6 Robin Barrow *Plato, Utilitarianism and Education* (London: Routledge and Kegan Paul, 1975) ch. 5
7 John Kleinig 'The fourth chapter of Mill's Utilitarianism' *Australasian Journal of Philosophy* (August 1970)

8 Happiness, Schooling and Education

1 See Robin Barrow *Common Sense and the Curriculum* (London: Allen & Unwin, 1976) Pt 2
2 R.F. Dearden 'Happiness and education' *The Philosophy of Education Society of Great Britain: Proceedings of the Annual Conference* (1967) p. 27
3 See for example Lynette Long and Susan Coleman 'The effect of various student problems and emotions on teacher response quality' *EDRS* (June 1976)
4 But this admission should not be confused with the suggestion that a sense of reality is unimportant in respect of acquiring happiness; see below 8.4
5 cf. Miriam Lewin Papanek 'Happiness is . . . ' paper presented at the Annual Convention of the New York State Psychological Association (May 1974) and Janice Porter Gump 'Sex-role attitudes and psychological well-being' *Journal of Social Issues* (Spring 1972)
6 I have explored the question of happiness in a totalitarian setting more fully in my *Plato, Utilitarianism and Education* (London: Routledge & Kegan Paul, 1975)
7 The need for most of the qualities mentioned here is recognised by Russell, although he does not make it clear why they are important; see above 3.8
8 See, for example, the *Republic* and above ch. 5
9 Russell *The Conquest of Happiness* (London: Allen & Unwin, 1975) p. 99
10 H. Schieser 'De-socialising school instead of deschooling society' paper presented at the National Convention of the American Educational Studies Association (October/November 1975)
11 See Rene Maheu 'Relations between sport and education' speech given

before the Scientific Congress convened by the organising committee for the Games of the 20th Olympiad (Munich, August 1972) and Brian Groombridge 'Sport' *Convergence* (1969)

12 In my *Plato, Utilitarianism and Education, op. cit.*

Select Bibliography

1 *Books*

ARISTOTLE *Nichomachean Ethics* (trans. J.A.K. Thomson, Harmondsworth: Penguin, 1953)

ASHTON, P. *et al. The Aims of Primary Education: A Study of Teachers' Opinions* (London: Macmillan, 1975)

BARROW, ROBIN *Plato, Utilitarianism and Education* (London: Routledge and Kegan Paul, 1975)

BARROW, ROBIN *Moral Philosophy for Education* (London: Allen and Unwin, 1975)

BARROW, ROBIN *Common Sense and the Curriculum* (London: Allen and Unwin, 1976)

BENTHAM, JEREMY *The Principles of Morals and Legislation* (New York: Hafner, 1948)

BRADBURN, N. and CAPLOVITZ, D. *Reports on Happiness* (Chicago: Aldine, 1965)

BRONFENBRENNER, URIE *Two Worlds of Childhood: USA and USSR* (London: Allen and Unwin, 1971)

CANTRIL, H. *The Pattern of Human Concerns* (New Brunswick: Rutgers University Press, 1965)

Children and Their Primary Schools A report of the Central Advisory Council for Education (England) (London: HMSO, Vol. 1, 1967) (Plowden)

COWAN, J.L. *Pleasure and Pain* (London: Macmillan, 1968)

FEINBERG, JOEL (ed.) *Moral Concepts* (London: Oxford University Press, 1969)

FREEDMAN, J. *Happy People: What Happiness Is, Who Has It and Why* (New York: Harcourt, Brace, 1979)

FROMM, ERICH *Fear of Freedom* (London: Routledge and Kegan Paul, 1942)

HALL, E.M. and DENNIS, L.A. *Living and Learning* (Toronto: Ontario Department of Education, 1968)

HSU, FRANCIS L.K. *Americans and Chinese: Reflections on Two Cultures and Their People* (New York: Doubleday, 1972)

KURTZ, PAUL *Exuberance: A Philosophy of Happiness* (Buffalo and New York City: Prometheus Books, 1977)

MILL, J.S. *see* M. Warnock (ed.)

NEILL, A.S. *Summerhill* (Harmondsworth: Penguin, 1968)

PLATO, *The Republic* (trans. Desmond Lee, Harmondsworth: Penguin, 1974)

PLOWDEN, *see, Children and Their Primary Schools*

ROBINSON, JOHN P. and SHAVER, PHILLIP R. *Measures of Social Psychological Attitudes* Ann Arbor, Michigan: Institute for Social Research, 1978)

ROUSSEAU, J.J. *Emile* (trans. Barbara Foxley, London: Everyman, Dent, 1972)

RUSSELL, BERTRAND *The Conquest of Happiness* (London: Allen and Unwin, 1975)

WARNOCK, M. (ed.) *Utilitarianism: John Stuart Mill* (London: Collins, The Fontana Library, 1962)

WESSMAN, E. and RICKS, D. *Mood and Personality* (New York: Holt, Rinehart and Winston, 1966)

WOLMAN, B.B. (ed.) *Handbook of General Psychology* (New Jersey: Prentice-Hall, 1973)

VON WRIGHT, G.H. *Varieties of Goodness* (London: Routledge and Kegan Paul, 1963)

2 *Philosophical papers*

ANSCOMBE, G.E.M. 'On the grammar of enjoy' *Journal of Philosophy* 64 (May 1967) pp. 607-14

AUSTIN, JEAN 'Pleasure and Happiness' *Philosophy* 43 (January 1968) pp. 51-62

BARROW, ROBIN 'Being and feeling happy' *Proceedings of the American Philosophy of Education Society* (1978)

BARROW, ROBIN 'On happiness' paper delivered at Annual Conference of the Philosophy of Education Society of Great Britain (1976)

BENDITT, THEODORE 'Happiness' *Philosophical Studies* 25 (January 1970) pp. 1-20 January 1974

BERTMAN, MARTIN A. 'Pleasure and the two happinesses in Aristotle' *Apeiron* 6 (Summer 1972) pp. 30-36

BILLINGS, JOHN R. 'J.S. Mill's quantity—quality distinction' *Mill News Letter* 7 (Fall 1971) pp. 6-16

BROCK, DAN W. 'Recent work in Utilitarianism' *American Philosophical Quarterly* (1973) pp. 241-76

BRONAUGH, R.N. 'The utility of quality' *Canadian Journal of Philosophy* (December 1974) pp. 317-25

BRONAUGH, R.N. 'The quality in pleasures' *Philosophy* (July 1974) pp. 320-2

BROYER, JOHN ALBIN 'Aristotle: is happiness ambiguous?' *Midwest Journal of Philosophy* (Spring 1973) pp. 1-5

CAMPBELL, RICHMOND 'The pursuit of happiness' *Personalist* (Autumn 1973) pp. 325-37

CHATTEGEE, MARGARET 'Some reflections on the concept of happiness' *Indian Philosophical Quarterly* (April 1977) pp. 313-18

DAHL, NORMAN O. 'Is Mill's hedonism inconsistent?' *American Philosophical Quarterly* (1973) pp. 37-54

DEARDEN, R.F. 'Happiness and education' *The Philosophy of Education Society of Great Britain: Proceedings of the Annual Conference* (1967) pp. 17-29

DEARDEN, R.F. 'On happiness: reply to R. Barrow' unpublished paper delivered at Annual Conference of Philosophy of Education Society of Great Britain (1976)

DUFF, ANTHONY 'Must a good man be invulnerable' *Ethics* (July 1976) pp. 294-311

FUCHS, ALAN E. 'The production of pleasure by stimulation of the brain: an alleged conflict between science and philosophy' *Philosophy and Phenomenological Research* (July 1976) pp. 494-505

GAUTHIER, DAVID P. 'Progress and happiness: a utilitarian reconsideration' *Ethics* (1967) pp. 77-82

GOLDSTEIN, IRWIN 'Happiness: the role of non-hedonic criteria in its evaluation'

International Philosophical Quarterly 13 (December 1973) pp. 523-34
HALLETT, GARTH 'Happiness' *The Heythrop Journal* (July 1971) pp. 301-3
KENNY, ANTHONY 'Happiness' *Proceedings of the Aristotelian Society* 66 (1965/6) pp. 93-102
KLEINIG, JOHN 'The fourth chapter of Mill's Utilitarianism' *Australasian Journal of Philosophy* (August 1970) pp. 197-205
LACHS, JOHN 'Two views of happiness in Mill' *Mill News Letter* (Fall 1973) pp. 16-20
MCPECK, JOHN 'Can Robin Barrow be happy and not know it?' *Proceedings of the American Philosophy of Education Society* (1978)
MAHOWALD, MARY 'Freedom versus happiness and "Women's lib" *Journal of Social Philosophy* (April 1975) pp. 10-13
MONTAGUE, ROGER 'Happin ss' *Proceedings of the Aristotelian Society* 67 (1966-67) pp. 87-102
NOREN, STEPHEN J. and DAVIS, ARLIS 'Pitcher on the awfulness of pain' *Philosophical Studies* 25 (February 1974) pp. 117-22
PITCHER, GEORGE 'The awfulness of pain' *Journal of Philosophy* (July 1970) pp. 481-91
PUCCETTI, ROLAND 'The sensation of pleasure' *British Journal of Philosophy and Science* 20 (1969) pp. 239-45
RESCHER, NICHOLAS 'The environmental crisis and the quality of life' in W.T. Blackstone (ed.) *Philosophy and the Environmental Crisis* (Athens: University of Georgia, 1974)
RUTHERFORD, LEWIS 'Notes on educational theory' *Journal of West Virginia Philosophical Society* (Fall 1974) pp. 18-20
SIMPSON, ROBERT W. 'Happiness' *American Philosophical Quarterly* (April 1975) pp. 169-76
SOLOMON, ROBERT C. 'Is there happiness after death?' *Philosophy* 51 (April 1976) pp. 189-93
LLOYD THOMAS, D.A. 'Happiness' *Philosophical Quarterly* 18 (71) (April 1968) pp. 97-113
WILSON, JOHN 'Happiness' *Analysis* 29 (1968) pp. 13-21

3 *Empirical research papers, etc. (including unpublished PhD dissertations)*

ARSCOTT, A 'Univariate statistics describing a nationwide sample of tenth grade boys' *Interim Report, Working Paper No. 2* (Ann Arbor, Michigan: Institute for Social Research, July 1968)
BAILEY, STEPHEN K. 'Educational purpose and the pursuit of happiness' *Phi Delta Kappan* (September 1976) pp. 42-7
BLAI, BORIS JNR 'Two year college faculties: their values and perceptions and Values and Perceptions of public and private junior college students' (Harcum Junior College, Pa: Report No: IRR-73-14)
BLAI, BORIS, JNR 'Two year college faculties: their values and perceptions and Values and Perceptions of public and private junior college students' (Harcum Junior College, Pa: Report No: IRR-73-14)
BLAZER, DAN and PALMORE, ERDMAN 'Religion and aging in a longitudinal panel' *Gerontologist* (February 1976) pp. 82-5
BUTLER, BROADUS N. 'The pursuit of happiness not pleasure' *Crisis* (May 1976) pp. 172-7
BUTLER, DONALD CARROLL 'An Analysis of the values and value systems reported by students, the general public, and educators in a selected

Appalachian public school district' PhD dissertation (Michigan State University, 1973)

CAMERON, PAUL 'Mood as an indicant of happiness: age, sex, social class and situational differences' *Journal of Gerontology* (March 1975) pp. 216-24

CAMPBELL, D. 'Social attitudes and other acquired behavioural dispositions' in S. Koch (ed.) *Psychology: a Study of a Science* (New York: McGraw-Hill, 1963)

CONSTANTINOPLE, ANNE 'Some correlates of average level of happiness among college students' *Developmental Psychology* (May 1970)

DAVIDSON RALPH P. 'Education in a changing economy' *Education Tomorrow* No. 6 (College Entrance Examination Board, New York, 1975)

'Educating our children for life, liberty and the pursuit of happiness' *Journal of Teacher Education* (Winter 1976) pp. 298-9

ELLIS, ALBERT 'The biological basis of human irrationality' paper presented at the Annual Meeting of the American Psychological Association (August/September 1975)

ELLIS, ALBERT 'Creative joy and happiness: the humanistic way' *Humanist* (January 1975) pp. 11-13

ERVIN, SAM J., JNR 'The pursuit of happiness' *NASSP Bulletin* (May 1977) pp. 128-35

EVANS, WAYNE O. 'Mind-altering drugs and the future' *Futurist* (June 1971) pp. 101-4

FAIRFIELD, ROY P. 'To saw a board' *Humanist* January/February 1975) pp. 37-9

FELLOWS, E 'A study of factors related to happiness' *Journal of Educational Research* (1956) pp. 231-4

FARMER, CAPEN 'Words and feelings: a developmental study of the language of emotion in children' PhD dissertation (Columbia University, 1967)

GILLISPIE, PHILIP H. *Learning Through Simulation Games* (New Jersey: *Paulist Press,* 1973)

GOLDHAMMER, KEITH 'Curriculum imperatives for meaningful education' *OSSC Bulletin* 20 (8) (April 1977)

GREEN R. 'On the measurement of mood' *Technical Report No. 10* (University of Rochester, 1965)

GROOMBRIDGE, BRIAN 'Sport' *Convergence* (1969) pp. 61-5

GUMP, JANICE PORTER 'Sex-role attitudes and psychological well-being' *Journal of Social Issues* (Spring 1972) pp. 79-92

HANTULA, JAMES 'Are angels really necessary for child-development?' *Journal of Thought* (January 1977) pp. 33-7

Institute for Social Research Newsletter (2) (University of Michigan: Summer 1974) 'Measuring the quality of life in America'

JOKIEL, BERNARD JOSEPH and STARKEY, JOHN 'Effect of a school-within-a-school program on attitudes of underachieving students' *EDRS* (1972)

KRAMER, HOWARD C. *et al.* 'Student concerns and sources of assistance' *Journal of College Student Personnel* (September 1974) pp. 389-93

LANDRY, RICHARD G. and PARDEW, E. MICHELLE 'Self-concept enhancement of preschool children' paper presented at the Annual Meeting of the American Educational Research Association (New Orleans: February 1973)

LAZARSFELD, PAUL F. 'The American Soldier — an expository review' *Public Opinion Quarterly* 13 (Fall 1949) pp. 377-404

LONG, LYNETTE and COLEMAN SUSAN 'The effect of various student problems and emotions on teacher response quality' *EDRS* (June 1976)

McCLOSKY, H. and SCHAER, J. 'Psychological dimensions of anomy' *American Sociological Review* (1965) pp. 14-40

McCORD ARLINE SAKUMA 'Happiness as educational equality' *Society* (November-December 1974) pp. 65-71

MACLEOD GORDON A. 'Does creativity lead to happiness and more enjoyment of life?' *Journal of Creative Behavior* (4th Quarter 1973) pp. 227-30

MAHEU, RENE 'Relations between sport and education' speech given before the Scientific Congress convened by the Organising Committee for the Games of the 20th Olympiad (Munich: August 1972)

'The Mood of American Youth' National Association of Secondary School Principals (Washington D.C.: 1974)

MOSHER, CRAIG 'Woodworker' *The Humanist* (January/February 1975) pp. 36-7

NOLL, E and BRADBURN, N. 'Work and happiness' paper presented at the 63rd Annual Meeting of the American Sociological Association (Boston: September 1968)

PAPADATOS, STEVEN P. 'Color them motivated — color's psychological effects on students' *NASSP Bulletin* (February 1973) pp. 92-4

PAPANEK, MIRIAN LEWIN 'Happiness is . . . correlates of academic satisfaction among undergraduates. The senior satisfaction survey of the class of 1972' paper presented at the Annual Convention of the New York State Psychological Association (May 1974)

PARDUCCI, ALLEN 'Grades, standards and happiness' *UCLA Educator* (Winter 1976) pp. 28-32

ROBINSON, J 'Occupational norms and differences in job satisfaction' in J. Robinson, R. Athanasiou and K. Head *Measures of Occupational Attitudes and Occupational Characteristics* (Ann Arbor, Michigan: Institute for Social Research, 1969)

SCHIESER, HANS A. 'De-socialising school instead of deschooling society' paper presented at the National Convention of the American Educational Studies Association (October/November 1975)

SIMMONS, J. 'Some intercorrelations among "Alienation" measures' *Social Forces* (1966) pp. 370-2

STEWART, ROBERT A.C. 'Satisfaction in stages of the life-cycle, levels of general hapiness and frequency of peak experience' *Social Behaviour and Personality* (1976) pp. 105-8

STRONG, WILLIAM 'Unself' *Media and Methods* November 1974)

TUSSING, A. DALE 'Campus disaffection, present and future' paper prepared for the Educational Staff Seminar on Alternatives in Post Secondary Education, Syracuse University Research Corporation (New York, 1971)

WESSMAN, D. 'A psychological inquiry into satisfaction and happiness' unpublished doctoral dissertation (Princeton University, 1956)

WILSON, W. 'An attempt to determine some correlates and dimensions of hedonic tone' unpublished doctoral dissertation (Northwestern University, 1960)

WILSON, W. 'Correlates of Avowed Happiness' *Psychological Bulletin* 67 (1967) pp. 294-306

Index

advertising, 127, 139
aesthetic satisfaction, 3, 8, 94
aggression, 10, 11, 136
alienation, 6, 7, 12, 36, 94, 98, 108
  see also anxiety, security
America (compared with China), 6, 98
  see also happiness, levels of
animals, 18, 48, 72
anomy, *see* anxiety
Anouilh, J., 30
Anscombe, G.E.M., 19
anxiety, 3, 5, 10, 12, 37, 73, 91, 94, 102, 104, 110, 114, 126, 135
  see also alienation, security
Archytas, 31
Aristotle, 3, Ch. 2, 31, 40, 43, 48-9 64, 68, 74, 83, 114, 128, 135
  on the contemplative life, 22-3
  on death and happiness, 23-5
  on happiness as the supreme end, 19-20
  on the nature of happiness, 15-19
asceticism, 44
Ashton, P., 2
Austin, Jean, 46, 68, 88, 108, 109
Austin, J.L., 31
Aurelius, Marcus, 40
authoritarianism, 10, 134

Bailey, S.K., 3, 5, 8, 15, 94, 95, 96, 97
Balinsky, B., 8
Barry, B., 68
Beatles, 39
Benditt, Th., 30, 52-4, 64, 79
Bentham, J., 3, 43
Blai, B., 113
Boethius, 41
Bradburn, N., 81
Bronfenbrenner, U., 98
Broyer, J.A., 22
Butler, B., 2, 6, 98-100
Butler, D.C., 113
Butler, S., 30, 36, 75

Cambridge, R.O., 35
Camus, A., 29
Cantril, H., 12
Caplovitz, D., 81
Carroll, L., 64
children, 18, 48, 54, 72, 96, Ch. 8
China (compared with America), 6, 98
choice, 6, 17, 100, 115, 116
Christie, A., 30, 132
Cicero, 31
colour, 4, 8, 134
competition, 36-7, 134-5, 138
concepts, 61-6
conceptual analysis, *see* philosophical analysis
Conrad, J., 32
consciousness, 72-3, 75, 76, 79, 81, 100, 109
Constantinople, A., 101
contemplative life, 18, 22-3, 26, 48
contentment, 34, 35, 37, 40, 42, 44, 47, 54, 66, 67, 72, 74, 79-80
convergers, 105
creativity, 3, 4, 8, 94, 102, 103

Davidson, R., 101
Davis, A., 110
Dearden, R.F., 29, 31, 50, 62, 114, 122, 123
death, 23-5, 32, 56
De Bono, E., 33
Dekker, T., 34
delusion, 29, 71, 74, 78, 84, 85, 87
democracy, 7, 78, 99, 100, 130, 131, 138
depression, *see* anxiety

desires, 16, 17, 18, 25, 34, 43, 47, 49, 52, 55, 66, 72, 75, 83, 117
determination, 131 ff.
Dewey, J., 3
drink, 37, 54, 130
Dryden, J., 34, 37
drugs, 5, 8, 46, 48, 54, 89, 108-12, 130, 137

economic benefit, 99
education, 1-5, 13, 38, 39, 64, 65, 96, 107, Ch. 8
emotions, 9, 37, 49, 75-6, 88-90
empathy, 131 ff.
empirical research (problems in), 4, 7, 8, 9, 11, 12, 25, 44, 67, 68, 101-2, 103-5
enmeshment, 74-5, 77, 79, 80, 84, 89, 90, 98, 100, 101, 102, 103, 105, 106, 109, 115, 116, 119, 131, 132, 135, 138, 140
  see also equilibrium, harmony
environment, *see* surroundings
Epicetus, 40
Epicurus, 40-1, 44, 52, 54, 107
equilibrium, 40, 41, 44, 75, 79, 106
  see also enmeshment, harmony
Erasmus, 33, 140
Ervin, S.J., 2, 97-8
escapism, 127-8
Euripides, 32
Evans, W.O., 108
expectations, 34, 54, 78, 94, 104, 105, 106, 107-8, 126-8, 131, 134, 139

failure, 106
family life, 5, 10, 13, 36, 38, 68, 74, 84, 85, 86, 87, 98, 101, 104-6, 113, 115
Feather, W., 33
Finkelman, J.H., 8
fortune, 18, 22, 24, 31, 61-2
freedom, 2, 5, 42, 55, 72, 78, 94, 95-8, 115, 116, 120, 129-30, 134
friendship, 15, 17, 18, 26, 35, 38, 55, 68, 69, 114, 128
Fromm, E., 39, 98
Fuchs, A.E., 111

games, 11, 136

Geach, P.T., 19
Gellner, E., 31
Goldstein, I., 55-6, 68, 70, 71, 84, 85
Graham, K., 31
Gray, T., 32

Hallet, G., 30
happiness
  as an aim of education, 3-4, Ch.8
  being and feeling, distinction between, 33, 48, 53, 87-92
  a broad concept, 64-5
  comparative judgements concerning, 30, 54-5, 79, 84
  contradictory of unhappiness, 37, 44, 52, 80-2
  control of, 37, 42, 45, 94, 109, 112, 130-3, 137
  criteria of, 46-8, 53, 72-3, 89
  a degree word, 65-6, 74, 75, 79, 83, 84
  different senses of, 62-4
  as an end, 16, 18, 19, 20, 35, 41, 43, 48-9, 51, Ch. 7
  judgements concerning, 45-6, 50-3, 70, 76-7, 83-87
  levels of, 6, 7, 12, 98, 107
  logically incompatible with, 73
  material conditions and, 46, 55, 68-71, 84, 138
  mistakes in attribution of, 33, 45-6, 48, 51-3, 77, 83-93
  nature of, 8, 13, 34, 38, 41, 42, 43, 45, 140, Chs. 2, 4, 5
  personal characteristics and, 13, 46, 48, 71
  prediction of, 46, 85, 86, 90-1
  uses of word, 50-1, 62-3
  value of, 1, 3, 4, 35, 36, 43, 123, Ch. 7
Hardie, W.F.R., 21
Hare, R.M., 46, 48, 52-3, 68, 70, 71, 72
harmony, 36, 98, 126, 135
  see also enmeshment, equilibrium
health, 10, 13, 17, 21, 42, 48, 55, 68, 69, 104, 128
Herodotus, 24
Herzberg, J., 9
Hobbes, T., 41
Horace, 33
Houston, B.K., 102

Hsu, F.L.K., 98
Hutcheson, F. 35
Huxley, A., 29, 33
hygeines, 9, 10, 129

Ibsen, H., 29
individual-centred upbringing, 6, 98
indoctrination, 72, 78
intelligence, 10, 15, 20, 23, 71, 94, 106, 131, 136, 137
intelligibility test, 70-1, 80-1, 82, 86
interest, 132
irrationality (biological basis for), 6

James, H., 31
job satisfaction, 9, 10, 13, 101, 104, 106, 137
Johnson, S., 30, 35
Jokiel, B.J., 9, 101, 134
Jonson, B., 35
joy, 32, 35, 37, 40, 66-7, 72, 80
Juvenal, 32

Kant, I., 42
Katzell, J., 10
Kenny, A., 46, 49
Kleinig, J., 118-9
knowledge, 6, 17, 32, 42, 78, 90, 123, 127, 129, 131, 133, 136
Kramer, H.C., 3, 8, 101, 102

Landry, R.G., 9, 102
Lazarsfeld, P.F., 103-4
Leggett, J., 12
Lenski, B., 12
linguistic analysis, *see* philosophical analysis
linguistic test, *see* intelligibility test
literature, 5, 6, 127, Ch. 3
  and philosophy, 28-31
Locke, J., 41-3
loneliness, 73, 74
love, 5, 64, 65, 68-9, 73, 74, 75, 76, 79, 81, 88, 101

McCord, A.S., 3
MacIntyre, A., 43
MacLeod, G.A., 4, 8, 102
McPeck, J., 88-90
marriage, *see* family life
Mathiasen, G., 102
Melzack, R., 110
mental defectives, 46, 56, 68, 70, 72
Mill, James, 3
Mill, J.S., 33, 43, 51, 96, 98, 117-9, 132
Milton, J., 35
moderation, 15, 26
modesty, 10, 38, 106, 131 ff.
Montague, R., 47, 52, 56, 66, 80, 127
Montesquieu, 33
Mosher, C., 7
motivators, 9, 10, 129
Murdoch, I., 31

needs, *see* desires
Neill, A.S., 2, 3, 98
Nietzsche, F., 85
Noren, S., 110

open-mindedness, 131 ff.
open society, *see* democracy
overachievers, 106
Ovid, 32

pain, 109-112
Papadatos, S., 4, 8, 134
Partridge, E., 27
philosophical analysis
  nature of, 20-2, 25-6, 28-31, 56, 61-4, 69, 70-1, 79-81
  need for, 8, 25-6, 40, 68, 74
Pitcher, G., 109-110
Plato, 3, 34, 74, 98, 136
pleasure, 5, 17, 18, 21, 34, 40, 42, 43, 47, 66, 77, 82-3, 96, 98, 101, 109-112, 140
Plowden report, 2
Pope, A., 35, 64
Prichard, H., 21-2
Puccetti, R., 109-111

Randall, J.H., 30
rationality, 18, 26, 32, 34, 37, 42, 133, 137
realism, 17, 74, 78, 87, 90, 94, 105, 107, 125, 126-8, 131, 137, 138
religion, 5, 103, 106, 107, 116
research, *see* empirical research
Rescher, N., 12, 30, 107-8
resignation, 33, 39, 41, 78, 131 ff.
responsibility, 6, 99, 101

Rousseau, J-J., 3, 75
Russell, B., 36-9, 42, 68, 100, 133, 134, 139
Rutherford, L., 3

satisfaction, 53-4
 see also contentment
Schacter, S., 109
Scheiser, H., 98, 101
schooling, 4, 113, Ch. 8
Schopenhauer, A., 42
Scott, J.P., 10
security, 6, 18, 32, 37, 38, 98, 101, 126-8, 129, 130, 138
 see also alienation, anxiety
self-absorbtion, 36
self-esteem, 5, 9, 10, 12, 17, 38, 73, 102, 105, 106, 126-8, 134, 138, 139
selfishness, 17, 48, 69, 71, 102
Seneca, 31, 32, 40, 41
sex, 5, 68, 82-3, 101
Shakespeare, W., 33, 75, 132
Shaw, B., 33, 35
Sidgwick, H., 47
simple life, 32-3
Simpson, R.W., 55, 66, 68, 70, 71, 83
simulation games, 6, 135
Singer, J., 109
Snow, C.P., 29
social-centred upbringing, 6, 98
Solomon, R.C., 25
Solon, 23, 32
Sophocles, 32
stoicism, 40-1
streaming, 137
Strong, W., 6, 102, 128
subconscious, 89-90
success, 9, 38, 101
surroundings, 4, 9, 10, 16-18, 37, 38, 48, 107, 133-4

Tennyson, A., 35
Theognis, 32
Thomas, D.A. Lloyd, 49-52, 62, 63, 75, 76, 85, 87
Tolstoy, L., 31, 35
totalitarianism, 6, 37, 79, 98, 131, 134, 138

Understanding, *see* knowledge
'unself' programme, 6, 7, 102, 128
utilitarianism, 35, 41-3, 44, 52, 54, 79, 98, 122-3, Ch. 7

Vaughan, H., 32
Vauvenargues, Marquis de, 33
virtue, 3, 15-18, 22, 24, 31, 34, 42, 48, 68, 74, 94-7, 116, 140
Von Wright, G.H., 44-6, 50, 52, 73, 79, 90, 130
Vroom, J., 10

Wall, P.D., 110
wants, 49, 54-5, 66, 83, 115
 see also desires
wealth, 5, 10, 13, 17, 18, 21, 26, 34, 35, 38, 48, 55, 68, 69, 75, 101, 104, 114, 140
Wessman, D., 12
Wilson, J., 48-9, 50, 55, 62, 66, 70, 71, 83
Wilson, W., 10, 82, 106
wisdom, 32, 33, 34, 75, 140
 see also intelligence
Wordsworth, W., 34
Wotton, H., 34

Young, P.T., 10, 134

Zeno 40